500

casseroles

500

casseroles

the only casserole compendium you'll ever need

Rebecca Baugniet

SELLERS

PUBLISHING

A Quintet Book

Published by Sellers Publishing, Inc.
161 John Roberts Road, South Portland, Maine 04106
For ordering information:
(800) 625-3386 Toll Free
(207) 772-6814 Fax
Visit our Web site: www.sellerspublishing.com • E-mail: rsp@rsvp.com

ISBN: 978-1-4162-0769-6
QTT.FHCA

This book was designed and produced by
Quintet Publishing Limited
6 Blundell Street
London N7 9BH
United Kingdom

Project Editor: Robert Davies
Copy Editor: Cary Hull
Photography: Ian Garlick
Food Styling: Gizzi Erskine
Editorial Assistant: Tanya Laughton
Art Director: Michael Charles
Managing Editor: Donna Gregory
Publisher: James Tavendale

10 9 8 7 6 5 4 3 2

Printed in China by SNP Leefung Printers Ltd.

contents

introduction

Casseroles are the original meal-in-one, the perfect comfort food. Think of "comfort" as tasty, filling, familiar, and warming (how many of us crave a hearty macaroni and cheese casserole on a cold winter night?). Casseroles are all that, as well as easy to eat, easy to prepare, easy on the budget, and easy to vary with just a few different ingredients. They are also easy to transport to welcome new neighbors or provide comfort for a friend in need.

For those seeking to provide a nutritious, balanced meal that doesn't take all day to make and won't use every pot in the kitchen, casseroles offer the perfect solution. Most casseroles can be divided into a series of small tasks, each one taking no more than a few minutes. If you are in a hurry, you may wish to skip a step, by using a prepared tomato sauce or substituting a can of condensed cream of mushroom or chicken soup for a white sauce. Often a casserole can be prepared completely in advance, which is another reason why they are so popular. For instance, a coq au vin can be made a day before you plan to serve it. It'll only require simple reheating, and keeping it for a day will only improve its flavor.

Casseroles make us additionally comfortable because they're economical; often casseroles showcase less expensive cuts of meat, which are all the tastier for having been braised, simmered, or stewed at length. Because a casserole offers the promise of a meal-in-one, it does not require any elaborate side dishes. Uncomplicated accompaniments, such as a crusty loaf of bread or a salad of mixed greens with a simple vinaigrette, are wonderful, low-preparation complements to any casserole.

Casseroles take their name from the French earthenware dish they've been associated with since the 1700s, but the practice of stewing meat and vegetables is ancient. Such dishes have been created and enjoyed around the globe for centuries — think of Moroccan tagine or Hungarian goulash. It seems that every region on Earth has had its own special way of combining meat and vegetables with some liquid and herbs to achieve delicious culinary results. This ancient way of preparing food is seeing a renaissance among today's chefs and home cooks alike. As the pendulum swings away from the highly detailed presentation of intensively executed dishes, we are seeing a new appreciation for traditional rural and rustic fare. Without pretension or fussiness, casseroles offer up what we truly crave — comfort food in all its glory. Casseroles are also gaining popularity with the rise of the "slow food" movement. Slow food does not imply endless hours spent in the kitchen; instead, it honors local food traditions and renews interest in the food we eat, how it tastes, and how our food choices impact the rest of the world.

Providing an updated look at a classic food, the dishes in this book may not be traditionally referred to as a "casserole." The word is now commonly used to describe both the cooking dish that goes from oven to table and the food made and served in these dishes. Almost all the recipes in this book adhere to this definition, although some may be known by other names such as risottos or stews. With only a few exceptions, however, the casseroles in this book involve a delicious combination of ingredients, often bound by a cream- or stock-based sauce and finished with a breadcrumb or cheese topping, and for the most part, suggesting the possibility of a meal in one dish. Most require only a short preparation time. They are uncomplicated and delicious, and they lend themselves to large, happy gatherings. Whichever recipe you try first, when you take part in the time-honored process of casserole cooking, you are sure to enjoy the results.

equipment

casserole dishes & dutch ovens

Casserole dishes are generally made of glass, ceramic, or earthenware. The suggestion given in the recipes in this book regarding casserole size should be used merely as a guideline; if the recipe you are making fits the capacity of a different-shaped casserole in your collection, by all means use what you have. You could always use several smaller dishes instead of a single larger one, if that is what's available to you. (As a rule, casseroles will need the same baking time and temperature, regardless of the size dish they are cooked in). If you do not already own any casserole dishes, the most common one is the 9x13x2-inch dish, which is used for most lasagnas and many other baked casseroles. Baking time may vary slightly if the dish is smaller, larger, shallower, or deeper than the one suggested, or if you are using a thicker earthenware dish. Test to make sure your casserole is heated through before removing from the oven. Always ensure that pork reaches an internal temperature of 145°F; poultry must be cooked to an internal temperature of 165°F. Temperatures for beef and lamb are less critical, but do check that the meat is fully cooked before serving.

The casserole dishes used in this book are divided into three sizes. "Small" designates a 4- or 6-cup capacity dish, so 8-, 9-, or 10-inch pans or pie plates; small loaf pans and 6- or 7-inch soufflé dishes fall into this category. "Medium" denotes an 8- or 10-cup capacity dish, so 8x8x2-, 9x9x2-, and 11x7x1$\frac{1}{2}$-inch pans; 9x5x3-inch loaf pans; and 8-inch soufflé dishes fall into this category. Finally, "large" is a 12-cup or larger capacity, and includes the 9x13x2-inch dish already mentioned (up to 16-cup capacity) as well as 8x8x3$\frac{1}{2}$-inch and 10x10x4-inch pans. A Dutch oven is a large, heavy, lidded dish that goes from stovetop to oven. While a Dutch oven is not an essential piece of equipment, if you are following a recipe that calls for one, be certain that your cookware is ovenproof, or else transfer your dish from saucepan to a casserole dish before baking.

frying pans & saucepans

Different-sized frying pans and saucepans are used throughout the book. Heavy cast-iron frying pans are best for simmering sauces, but nonstick frying pans can also be used. Having a choice of two or three different sizes makes preparation of many casseroles easier.

mixing bowls, colanders, cutting boards, measuring cups & spoons

A variety of mixing bowls is essential in any kitchen. In casserole making, small and medium bowls are often used to make sauces or to hold ingredients until they need to be incorporated. A colander for draining pasta or cooked vegetables is equally useful. Every kitchen should have a minimum of two cutting boards—one for raw meat preparation and a second one for all other ingredients. Secondary ingredients in casseroles can be increased or decreased to accommodate tastes; however, core ingredients should be measured accurately for successful results. Correct measuring equipment is therefore important. Use calibrated measuring cups and proper measuring spoons.

other equipment

Other pieces of useful equipment for making casseroles include a variety of good knives, especially a paring knife and a chef's knife for chopping vegetables. A good cheese grater is indispensable, and a small glass or metal hand juicer is all that is needed for obtaining fresh citrus juice without the seeds. Spatulas are useful for scraping sauce out of saucepans, as well as for serving. Wooden spoons and whisks are essential for making smooth sauces, while an immersion blender can be a useful tool if you need to make a sauce extra-smooth. Since casseroles go directly from oven to table, trivets or placemats are required to protect your tabletop. In cooking, timing is extremely important. Either use the timer on your oven or invest in an inexpensive, accurate digital timer.

ingredients

meat, poultry & fish

Most of the meat, poultry, and fish used in these recipes can be found in all grocery stores; however, it is always preferable to patronize, when possible, a local butcher and fishmonger. Not only will you find a good variety (including organic) of meats and poultry and wild or responsibly farmed fish, these professionals will be able to direct you to the best cuts for your recipe. They know that by utilizing such methods as pot roasting, braising, and stewing — all common to casserole cooking — you can tenderize less expensive, tougher cuts of meats. Whole joints of meat, known as the silverside, rib, and brisket cuts of beef, shoulder, breast, and shank cuts of lamb, and leg, shoulder, belly, and hock cuts of pork, are boned and rolled, making them ideal for pot roasting. Braising often calls for whole steaks or chops, using shin, leg, or neck cuts of beef; shoulder steak cuts of lamb; and leg or shoulder steak cuts of pork. Stewing calls for cubed meat, using chuck or blade cuts of beef and shoulder or leg cuts of lamb. Ask your butcher or fishmonger for advice as well as assistance with any preparations, such as trimming or cutting, that need to be done.

vegetables

Canned whole tomatoes are used in most recipes, because seeds that have been crushed during processing add bitterness to the flavor. If you use canned chopped tomatoes, you may wish to add a bit of sugar to reduce the bitterness. Start with 1/4 teaspoon sugar and add more to taste. If making sauce from fresh tomatoes, opt for vine-ripened ones with a good, strong tomato aroma. Always use the freshest produce you can find. Patronizing local farmers and using seasonal produce will guarantee the best flavor as well as being environmentally responsible.

eggs
Large eggs are used in this book unless otherwise noted. Free-range and organic eggs have better flavor as well as being an environmentally friendly choice.

oil
Extra-virgin olive oil is used in this book unless otherwise noted. When vegetable oil is called for, canola oil or any light, neutral vegetable oil are preferred. One favorite is sunflower oil, which can be found in most grocery stores or health-food shops. Low-fat cooking spray is used in some of the light recipes and can be found in the baking aisle of most grocery stores, next to the other oils. Unsalted butter is used throughout the book unless otherwise noted.

flour
All-purpose flour is used in this book unless otherwise noted.

herbs & spices
Fresh herbs will guarantee the most flavorful sauces and toppings, but dried herbs are an acceptable substitute. A basic rule for herb substitutions is that 1 teaspoon freshly chopped herbs equals 1/4 teaspoon dried and crumbled herbs. A wide variety of spices is used in casseroles—cumin, coriander, turmeric, cardamom, and nutmeg are all widely available in grocery stores. Check health-food stores and specialty spice shops for more obscure spices.

stocks

Many casserole recipes call for beef, chicken, fish, or vegetable stock. Fresh, good-quality stock can be found in supermarkets, delicatessens, and food stores. It is also available in cans, cartons, cubes, and powder in the soup aisle of your market. Low-sodium stocks using organic ingredients will enhance the flavor of your casseroles and give you greater control over the amount of salt you want in your dish. Homemade stocks are easy to prepare and freeze well, so it is worth making a big batch and storing it in smaller quantities, ready for thawing and using in recipes. You can make stock from scratch, but the most flavorful chicken, beef, and fish stocks are made with the leftover bones or carcasses from roasts.

vegetable stock

2 onions, roughly chopped
2 carrots, roughly chopped
2 celery sticks, roughly chopped
1 bay leaf
2 sprigs fresh thyme

4 parsley stalks
1 tsp. whole black peppercorns
1/2 tsp. salt
6 cups water

Place all ingredients in a large saucepan and bring to a boil. Reduce heat to low, simmer for 1 hour, skimming off any foam that rises to the surface. Strain the stock through a fine sieve, then chill or freeze until ready to use.

Makes about 4 cups

chicken stock

1 chicken carcass
2 onions, roughly chopped
2 carrots, roughly chopped
2 celery stalks, roughly chopped

2 bay leaves
1 tsp. whole black peppercorns
1/2 tsp. salt
6 cups water

Place all ingredients in a large saucepan and bring to a boil. Reduce heat to low, simmer for 1 1/2 hours, skimming off any foam that rises to the surface. Strain the stock through a fine sieve, then chill or freeze until ready to use. Once stock has chilled, skim any fat that has congealed on the surface.

Makes about 4 cups

fish stock

1 lb. fish bones, without gills
1 onion, roughly chopped
1 leek, roughly chopped
2 celery stalks, roughly chopped
1 bay leaf

4 parsley stalks
1/2 tsp. whole black peppercorns
1/2 tsp. salt
4 1/2 cups water

Place fish bones in a large saucepan and add all remaining ingredients. Bring to a boil, then reduce heat to low and simmer for 30 minutes, skimming off any foam that rises to the surface. Strain the stock through a fine sieve, then chill or freeze until ready to use.

Makes about 4 cups

beef stock

2 lb. beef bones
1 onion, roughly chopped
1 leek, roughly chopped
2 carrots, roughly chopped
1 celery stalk, roughly chopped
1 bay leaf

2 sprigs fresh thyme
4 sprigs fresh parsley
1 tsp. whole black peppercorns
1/2 tsp. salt
6 cups water

Preheat oven to 425°F. Place bones in a roasting pan and roast for 40 minutes. Transfer bones to a large saucepan and add all remaining ingredients. Bring to a boil, reduce heat to low, and simmer for 3 hours, skimming off any foam that rises to the surface. Strain the stock through a fine sieve, then chill or freeze until ready to use. Once the stock has chilled, skim any fat that has congealed on the surface.

Makes about 4 cups

garnishes & condiments

Garnishes add flavor, texture, and visual appeal, making them an easy way to elevate a humble casserole to an elegant offering fit for guests. Many recipes in this book suggest appropriate garnishes, but do experiment to find your own favorite presentations. Finely chopped or shredded fresh herbs such as chives, basil, Italian parsley, mint, sage, and cilantro all look pretty as well as adding a flavor punch. Zested citrus peel or finely sliced scallions can be an effortless way to add zing to a dish, just as croutons or lightly toasted seeds (sesame, pumpkin, or sunflower) can contribute texture and nutrients to a meal. Condiments like salsas, relishes, chutneys, and hot sauce can offer an element of spice to milder casseroles, while plain yogurt, sour cream, tzatziki, or raita will balance out curries and other spicy dishes.

family feasts

When you are expecting a crowd, a hearty casserole

is a great way to satisfy everyone's appetite. The

recipes in this chapter are easy to assemble in

advance and reheat at dinnertime.

tamale casserole

see variations page 36

This tasty casserole evokes all the flavors of the Mexican dish that is traditionally steamed or baked in cornhusks.

2 tbsp. extra-virgin olive oil
1 1/2 lb. lean ground beef
1 cup finely chopped onion
1 garlic clove, minced
1/2 cup chopped red bell pepper
1 cup fine cornmeal
1 (28-oz.) can whole tomatoes, drained, with
    1/2 liquid reserved

1 cup corn kernels (fresh, canned, or frozen)
1 tbsp. chili powder
3 tsp. salt
1/4 tsp. freshly ground black pepper
1 1/2 cups whole milk
2 tbsp. unsalted butter
1 cup grated cheddar cheese
2 eggs, lightly beaten

Preheat oven to 375°F. Heat olive oil in large saucepan. Add ground beef and brown, about 7 minutes. Add onion, garlic, and red bell pepper, and cook for 5 minutes longer, until onion is translucent. In small bowl, combine 1 cup water with 1/2 cup cornmeal. Add cornmeal mixture to beef mixture, cover, and simmer for 10 minutes. Stir in tomatoes with reserved liquid; break up tomatoes into smaller pieces. Add corn, chili powder, 2 teaspoons salt, and pepper. Simmer for another 5 minutes, then transfer to a large (3-liter) casserole.

In medium saucepan, heat milk with remaining salt and butter. When milk is warm, slowly add remaining 1/2 cup cornmeal, stirring constantly. Continue to cook and stir over medium heat until mixture thickens. Remove from heat and add cheese and eggs. Spoon cornmeal mixture over meat mixture. Bake for 35–40 minutes, until topping is golden brown and casserole is heated through and bubbly. If making ahead, the filling can be made up to two days in advance and refrigerated. The topping is best eaten on the day it is made.

Serves 4–6

chicken tetrazzini

see variations page 37

The opera diva Luisa Tetrazzini was the inspiration for this dish, which is said to have been made for the first time at the Palace Hotel in San Francisco.

7 oz. uncooked spaghetti
5 tbsp. (1/2 stick) unsalted butter
1 carrot, chopped
1 celery stalk, chopped
1/2 cup all-purpose flour

salt and freshly ground black pepper to taste
2 cups chicken broth
2 cups whole milk
2 cups cooked chicken in bite-sized pieces
1 cup grated sharp cheddar cheese

Preheat oven to 350°F. Cook spaghetti according to package instructions. Drain and toss with 1 tablespoon butter. Set aside. In small saucepan, boil chopped carrot and celery in a small amount of water for 5 minutes. Drain and set aside.

To prepare the sauce, melt remaining butter in large saucepan over low heat. Add flour, salt, and pepper. Stir constantly, until mixture is smooth and bubbling. Continue stirring for 1 minute, then remove from heat. Whisk in broth and milk and return to stove. Bring mixture to boil, whisking constantly. Remove from heat once mixture has thickened, about 1–2 minutes after it comes to a boil. Stir in spaghetti, carrots, and celery. Pour into a large casserole and sprinkle grated cheddar on top. Bake for 25–30 minutes, until bubbly.

Serves 6

tortilla lasagna

see variations page 38

Delectable layers of tortillas, refried beans, seasoned ground beef, salsa, and melted cheese are sure to please in this dish inspired by the flavors of Mexico.

1 lb. lean ground beef	4 (9-inch) flour tortillas
1 cup prepared salsa	2 cups grated mild cheddar
1 tsp. ground cumin	sour cream for garnish
1 (19-oz.) can refried beans	chopped green onions for garnish

Preheat oven to 350°F. To prepare filling, brown ground beef in a large frying pan. Drain. Stir in salsa and cumin. Warm refried beans in saucepan over low heat until spreadable. Place one tortilla in ungreased 9-inch pie plate. Cover with half the beef mixture. Sprinkle with 1/2 cup grated cheese. Place another tortilla on top of the cheese. Spread half the refried beans over the tortilla. Sprinkle with another 1/2 cup grated cheese. Repeat these layers once more. Bake for 20 minutes, until cheese is melted and lasagna is heated through. Slice and garnish with sour cream and chopped green onions.

Serves 4–6

scalloped potatoes with prosciutto

see variations page 39

The bites of salty prosciutto found amidst slices of creamy potato elevate this casserole to new heights.

3 tbsp. unsalted butter
1/4 cup finely chopped onion
3 tbsp. all-purpose flour
salt and freshly ground black pepper to taste

2 1/2 cups whole milk
8 oz. prosciutto, cut into bite-sized pieces
2 lb. russet potatoes, peeled and finely sliced

Preheat oven to 350°F. Butter a large rectangular 9x13-inch casserole. Set aside.

To prepare the sauce, melt 3 tablespoons butter in large saucepan over low heat. Add chopped onions and sauté until translucent, about 5 minutes. Add flour, salt, and pepper. Stir constantly, until mixture is smooth and bubbling. Continue stirring for 1 minute, then remove from heat. Whisk in milk and return to stove. Bring mixture to boil, whisking constantly. Remove from heat when mixture has thickened, about 1–2 minutes after it comes to a boil. Stir in prosciutto.

Spread potato slices in casserole. Pour sauce over potatoes, ensuring that all potatoes are covered with sauce. Cover casserole with aluminum foil and bake for 30 minutes. Remove foil and continue cooking for 60–70 minutes, until potatoes are tender and browned at the edges. Allow to cool slightly before serving.

Serves 6

curried chicken with potatoes

see variations page 40

The separate flavors of lemon, ginger, and cilantro all shine in this beautiful chicken curry.

2 tbsp. freshly grated ginger
4 tbsp. water
2 1/2 lb. skinless, boneless chicken breasts, cut into bite-sized pieces
6 tbsp. canola oil
3 cloves garlic, minced
1 bunch fresh cilantro, finely chopped
1/4 tsp. cayenne

2 tsp. ground cumin
1 tsp. ground coriander
1/2 tsp. powdered turmeric
1 tsp. salt
2 tbsp. fresh lemon juice
2/3 cup water
3 russet potatoes, peeled and cubed

In a small bowl, combine ginger and 4 tablespoons water to form a paste. Set aside. In large pot or Dutch oven, brown chicken in batches in canola oil. Remove from pot and set aside with cooking juices. Add garlic to pot, and cook over medium heat until golden. Stir in ginger mixture and continue cooking for a minute. Add chopped cilantro, ground spices, and salt. Cook for another minute.

Return chicken and liquid to the pot. Add lemon juice, 2/3 cup water, and potatoes. Stir and allow curry to come to boiling point. Reduce heat to simmer, cover, and cook for 15 minutes, stirring occasionally to ensure that potatoes cook evenly. Check to make sure potatoes are cooked through. If not, continue simmering for 5 minutes longer, and then serve. If making in advance, prepare curry without adding potatoes. Half an hour before you are ready to serve, bring curry to a boil, add potatoes and proceed with recipe.

Serves 4–6

classic macaroni & cheese

see variations page 41

Everyone's number one comfort food. This is the classic retro recipe, complete with breadcrumbs and tomato slices. With so many possible variations you'll never be bored.

2 cups uncooked macaroni
1/4 cup chopped onion
1/4 cup unsalted butter
1/4 cup all-purpose flour
1/2 tsp. salt
1/4 tsp. freshly ground black pepper

1/4 tsp. Worcestershire sauce
2 cups whole milk
2 cups grated sharp white cheddar
6 slices fresh tomato
1/4 cup breadcrumbs

Preheat oven to 350°F. In a large pot of salted, boiling water, cook the macaroni for 9 minutes. The pasta should be barely al dente, as it will continue to cook in the oven.

As the pasta is cooking, prepare the cheese sauce. In large saucepan, sauté onion in butter over low heat until onion is soft and translucent, about 5 minutes. Add flour, salt, pepper, and Worcestershire sauce. Stir constantly, until mixture is smooth and bubbling. Continue stirring for 1 minute, then remove from heat. Whisk in milk and return to stove. Bring mixture to a boil, whisking continuously. When mixture has thickened, about 1–2 minutes after it comes to a boil, add cheese. Stir until blended and remove from heat.

Stir drained pasta into cheese sauce, making sure all the pasta is coated. Transfer to a large casserole. Arrange tomato slices over the macaroni and sprinkle breadcrumbs on top. Bake for 20–25 minutes, until breadcrumbs have browned and pasta is bubbly.

Serves 4–6

stuffed zucchini

see variations page 42

Zucchini takes on a new appeal when filled with a decadent stuffing.

8 medium-sized zucchini, cut in half lengthwise
1/2 cup finely chopped onion
2 tbsp. unsalted butter
1/4 cup finely chopped Italian parsley
3 cups cubed cooked ham

3 tbsp. sour cream
1 tbsp. Dijon mustard
salt and freshly ground black pepper to taste
1 1/2 cups grated Gruyère cheese

Preheat oven to 375°F. Butter a large rectangular casserole.

Using a metal spoon, scrape most of the flesh from each of the zucchini halves. Discard flesh.

In small frying pan, sauté onion in butter over low heat until onion is soft and translucent, about 5 minutes. Set aside.

In a medium-sized bowl, combine remaining ingredients except grated Gruyère. Stir in sautéed onions. Fill each zucchini half with 1/8 of the ham mixture. Arrange zucchini in baking dish and sprinkle with grated Gruyère. Bake for 25 minutes, finishing for 3 minutes under broiler if desired.

Serves 4

easy pot roast with sweet potatoes

see variations page 43

This meal-in-one will fill your home with an amazing aroma as it cooks.

1 envelope onion soup mix
1 1/2 cups water, plus 3 tbsp
1/4 cup soy sauce
2 tbsp. brown sugar
1 tsp. freshly grated ginger

1 3-lb. boneless pot roast (rump, chuck, or
   round roast)
4 sweet potatoes, peeled and cut into
2-inch chunks
2 tbsp. all-purpose flour

Preheat oven to 325°F. In Dutch oven or large, heavy, ovenproof pot with lid, combine soup mix, 1 1/2 cups water, soy sauce, brown sugar, and ginger. Place roast in pot, cover, and bake for 1 hour 45 minutes. Add sweet potatoes, cover, and return to oven for additional 45 minutes, until beef and potatoes are tender. Transfer roast and potatoes to serving platter. Reserve liquid in pot.

To make gravy, whisk flour with 3 tablespoons water in measuring cup. Pour flour mixture into reserved liquid and bring to a boil on stovetop, stirring frequently. Cook for 2 minutes, until gravy thickens. Serve with pot roast.

Serves 6

variations

tamale casserole

see base recipe page 21

tamale casserole with beans
Prepare the basic recipe, stirring 1 can of black beans, drained, into the
beef mixture before transferring to casserole dish.

tamale casserole with olives
Prepare the basic recipe, stirring 1/2 cup chopped pimiento-stuffed
olives into the beef mixture before transferring to casserole dish.

spicy tamale casserole
Prepare the basic recipe, adding 1 large jalapeño pepper, seeded and finely
chopped, with the seasonings. Increase chili powder to 2 tablespoons and
add 1 teaspoon ground cumin and 1/4 teaspoon ground allspice.

tamale casserole with cilantro
Prepare the basic recipe, adding 1/3 cup finely chopped fresh cilantro to
the beef mixture.

chicken tetrazzini

see base recipe page 22

tuna tetrazzini with mushrooms & olives
Prepare the basic recipe, omitting carrots and celery, and replacing chicken with 2 cups drained and flaked canned white tuna. Add 1 cup sliced olives and 1 cup sautéed sliced mushrooms.

chicken tetrazzini with orzo
Prepare the basic recipe, replacing spaghetti with an equal quantity of cooked orzo.

chicken tetrazzini with slivered almonds
Prepare the basic recipe, adding 1/2 cup slivered almonds to the sauce.

quick chicken tetrazzini
Prepare the basic recipe, omitting butter, flour, salt, pepper, chicken, and broth. In large casserole, combine 1 can condensed cream of mushroom soup, 1 can condensed cream of chicken soup, 3/4 cup milk, and 2 tablespoons dry white wine. Add cooked spaghetti, chicken, and vegetables, and bake as directed.

turkey tetrazzini
Prepare the basic recipe, replacing the cooked chicken with an equal quantity of cooked turkey.

variations

tortilla lasagna

see base recipe page 25

taco tortilla lasagna
Prepare the basic recipe, replacing cumin with a packet of taco seasoning.

tortilla lasagna with monterey jack
Prepare the basic recipe, replacing the mild cheddar with an equal quantity of grated Monterey Jack.

vegetarian tortilla lasagna
Prepare the basic recipe, replacing the cooked ground beef with 2 cups cooked white rice.

tortilla lasagna with cilantro
Prepare the basic recipe, replacing the chopped green onion garnish with chopped cilantro.

tortilla lasagna with italian sausage
Prepare the basic recipe, replacing the ground beef with 1 lb. mild Italian sausage, removed from its casings.

variations

scalloped potatoes with prosciutto

see base recipe page 26

basic scalloped potatoes
Prepare the basic recipe, omitting the prosciutto.

scalloped potatoes with ham
Prepare the basic recipe, replacing the prosciutto with an equal quantity of
chopped cooked ham.

scalloped potatoes with pancetta
Prepare the basic recipe, replacing the prosciutto with an equal quantity of
chopped pancetta.

scalloped potatoes with mushrooms
Prepare the basic recipe, adding 1 cup sliced cremini mushrooms to the
sliced potatoes in the buttered casserole.

lighter scalloped potatoes
Prepare the basic recipe, replacing the butter with margarine and the whole
milk with skim milk.

variations

curried chicken with potatoes

see base recipe page 29

curried chicken with potatoes & peas
Prepare the basic recipe, adding 1/2 cup fresh or frozen peas in
the last 5 minutes of cooking.

curried chicken with potatoes & carrots
Prepare the basic recipe, adding 1 cup peeled and chopped carrots with
the potatoes.

curried chicken with potatoes & mango chutney
Prepare the basic recipe, serving each portion with a dollop of prepared
mango chutney on top.

curried turkey with potatoes
Prepare the basic recipe, replacing the chicken with an equal quantity of
boneless, skinless turkey breast.

curried tofu with potatoes
Prepare the basic recipe, replacing the chicken with 2 pounds cubed extra-
firm tofu.

classic macaroni & cheese

see base recipe page 30

extra kid-friendly mac & cheese
Prepare the basic recipe, omitting onions, tomato slices, and breadcrumbs.
Substitute sharp orange cheddar for white cheddar.

macaroni & cheese with butternut squash
Prepare the basic recipe, omitting onion, tomato slices, and breadcrumbs. Prepare
butternut squash purée by roasting half a squash, flesh-side down, on a lightly
oiled baking sheet, in a 375°F oven for 35–40 minutes. When tender, mash
smooth and measure 1/2 cup. Add squash with the cheese, stir, and bake.

rigatoni & cheese with cauliflower
Prepare the basic recipe, replacing macaroni with al dente rigatoni. Add 1 cup
steamed cauliflower florets. Omit tomato slices and breadcrumbs.

chili macaroni
Prepare the basic recipe, omitting cheese sauce, tomatoes, and breadcrumbs. Stir
cooked pasta into 2 cups chili. Top with grated Monterey Jack before baking.

mac & cheese all grown up
Prepare the basic recipe, omitting tomatoes and breadcrumbs. Melt 3 tablespoons
unsalted butter in large skillet. Add 3 cups sliced shallots and season with salt
and pepper. Cover and cook until shallots are caramelized, 12–15 minutes. Spread
over pasta. Top with 2/3 cup crumbled chèvre. Bake as directed.

variations

stuffed zucchini

see base recipe page 32

stuffed yellow squash
Prepare the basic recipe, replacing the zucchini with an equal quantity
of yellow summer squash.

vegetarian stuffed zucchini
Replace the ham filling with a vegetarian filling. Reserve flesh from the
8 zucchini. Sauté 1 large onion, finely chopped; 1 clove garlic, minced;
1 cup chopped mushrooms; and reserved zucchini flesh in 2 tablespoons
unsalted butter for 5 minutes, until onions are translucent and vegetables are
tender. Season with 1/2 teaspoon basil, 1/4 teaspoon thyme, and salt and freshly
ground pepper to taste. In medium bowl, combine 3 eggs, 1 1/2 cups cottage
cheese, 1/4 cup wheat germ and 3 tablespoons tamari sauce. Add 1 cup grated
vegetarian cheddar and 1 cup cooked brown rice. Mix with sautéed vegetables and
stuff zucchini shells. Top with grated vegetarian swiss cheese and bake as directed.

crab-stuffed zucchini
Prepare the basic recipe, replacing the ham with 2 (8-oz.) cans crabmeat,
drained and flaked. Replace Gruyère with an equal quantity of mozzarella.

chicken-stuffed zucchini
Prepare the basic recipe, replacing the ham with an equal quantity of cubed,
cooked chicken.

easy pot roast with sweet potatoes

see base recipe page 35

easy pot roast with sweet potatoes & green beans
Prepare the basic recipe, adding 2 cups fresh green beans, topped and tailed, with the sweet potatoes.

easy pot roast with sweet potatoes, carrots & parsnips
Prepare the basic recipe, adding 3 large carrots and 3 large parsnips, peeled and cut into large chunks, with the sweet potatoes.

easy pot roast with russet potatoes
Prepare the basic recipe, replacing the sweet potatoes with 6 large russet potatoes, peeled and cut into 2-inch chunks.

easy pot roast with sweet potatoes & butternut squash
Prepare the basic recipe, adding 2 cups butternut squash, peeled and cut into 2-inch chunks, with the sweet potatoes.

pasta & rice casseroles

Nothing says comfort food like carbs—and these recipes deliver. Whether you are looking for a hearty main course, an interesting side dish, or just the right contribution for a potluck, you'll find it here.

red rice & beef

see variations page 64

Easy to make and easy to eat, this casserole takes its name from the tomato and pepper.

4 slices bacon
1 cup finely chopped onion
1 clove garlic, minced
1/2 cup finely chopped red bell pepper
1 lb. lean ground beef

1 cup uncooked basmati rice
1 (19-oz.) can whole tomatoes with liquid
1 tsp. salt
freshly ground black pepper to taste
1/2 cup grated cheddar cheese

Preheat oven to 350°F. Cook bacon in frying pan until crisp. Remove from pan, crumble, and place in medium (9x7-inch) rectangular casserole. Slide bacon pieces around dish to grease bottom and sides of casserole.

Sauté onion, garlic, and bell pepper in same frying pan until onion is translucent, about 5 minutes. Add ground beef and rice. Cook over medium heat until meat is browned. Add tomatoes with liquid, salt, and pepper. Break up tomatoes into smaller pieces and stir to combine. Transfer mixture to casserole. Top with grated cheddar. Cover with aluminum foil and bake for 45 minutes. Remove foil and continue baking for a further 15 minutes, or until rice is tender.

Serves 4–6

rigatoni & italian sausage bake

see variations page 65

This hearty casserole will feed a crowd or can be divided into two portions—one to eat, one to freeze for a busy night.

1 1/2 lb. mild Italian sausage
1 medium yellow onion, finely chopped
3 cloves garlic, minced
1 tsp. dried basil
1/2 tsp. dried oregano
1/4 tsp. dried thyme

salt and freshly ground black pepper to taste
1/2 cup tomato paste
2 (28-oz.) cans whole tomatoes with liquid
1 lb. uncooked rigatoni
2 cups grated provolone
1/4 cup finely chopped fresh Italian parsley

Remove sausage from casings to form small chunks. Brown sausage in large, heavy saucepan or Dutch oven over medium heat. Set browned sausage aside, and discard all but 2 tablespoons fat. Sauté onion, garlic, herbs, salt, and pepper until onion is translucent, about 5 minutes. Stir in tomato paste and continue cooking for 3 minutes. Add tomatoes with liquid. Break up tomatoes into smaller pieces and bring sauce to a boil. Return sausage to sauce and reduce heat to low. Simmer, uncovered, for 45 minutes, until sauce thickens.

Preheat oven to 375°F. In large pot of boiling salted water, cook pasta for 6 minutes, until al dente. Drain and add to sauce. Add 3/4 cup grated provolone and chopped parsley, and stir to combine. Transfer to a large (9x13-inch) rectangular casserole and top with remaining cheese. Cover casserole with aluminum foil and bake for 30 minutes, until hot and bubbly. Remove foil 10 minutes before the end of cooking to brown top of casserole.

Serves 6–8

three cheese & spinach baked manicotti

see variations page 66

This version of the popular baked pasta dish consists of a mouthwatering cheese and spinach filling, covered with a classic marinara sauce.

1/4 cup extra-virgin olive oil
2 garlic cloves, minced
1 (28-oz.) can plum tomatoes, drained
1/4 tsp. salt
8–10 fresh basil leaves, roughly chopped
20 oz. frozen spinach, thawed and drained

1 cup ricotta cheese
1 cup small-curd cottage cheese
1/3 cup freshly grated Parmesan, plus 3 tbsp.
pinch of freshly ground nutmeg
1/4 tsp. freshly ground black pepper
14 uncooked manicotti shells

To prepare marinara sauce, heat olive oil in large saucepan over medium heat. When oil is hot, add garlic and cook until golden, about 4 minutes. Add drained tomatoes and salt, breaking up tomatoes into smaller pieces. Bring to a simmer and cook for 15–20 minutes, stirring frequently, until sauce thickens. Add basil and set aside. Preheat oven to 350°F.

To make the filling, lightly press chopped spinach in a fine sieve to remove excess liquid. Pat dry with paper towel. Combine spinach, ricotta, cottage cheese, 1/3 cup Parmesan, nutmeg, and pepper. Spread 1 cup of sauce over bottom of a large (9x13-inch) casserole. Stuff each manicotti shell with spinach filling, and arrange over layer of sauce. Cover manicotti with remaining sauce and sprinkle with remaining Parmesan. Cover casserole with aluminum foil and bake for 1 1/2 hours, until sauce is bubbly and manicotti are tender and heated through. Remove foil 20 minutes before the end of cooking to brown top of casserole.

Serves 6–8

arroz con pollo

see variations page 67

This is the quintessential Spanish and Latin American casserole. There are many versions of arroz con pollo, but all begin with a sofrito—the base for a sauce made by sautéeing chopped onions, garlic, pepper, and spices in olive oil.

2 cups warm water
large pinch of saffron threads
1 tsp. Spanish paprika plus 1 tbsp.
3 cups uncooked Arborio rice
2 tbsp. extra-virgin olive oil
1 cup finely chopped onion
3 garlic cloves, minced
1/2 cup chopped red bell pepper
2 slices bacon, cut into small pieces

2 tsp. ground cumin
pinch of salt
1 (8-oz.) can plain tomato sauce
1 lb. boneless, skinless chicken breasts, cut into
    bite-sized pieces
1 (12-oz.) bottle pale ale
4 cups chicken stock
1 tsp. fresh lime juice
salt and freshly ground black pepper to taste

In measuring cup, combine warm water, saffron, and 1 teaspoon paprika. Place rice in medium-sized bowl and add saffron water. Stir to combine and set aside. To prepare the sofrito, heat olive oil over medium-high heat in a Dutch oven or a large heavy-based saucepan. Stir in onion, garlic, bell pepper, and bacon, and cook for 5 minutes, stirring often. Add cumin, remaining paprika, and salt, and continue to cook for additional 5 minutes. Add tomato sauce and chicken, stirring to coat all sides of chicken. Reduce heat to medium-low, cover, and cook for 15–20 minutes, stirring occasionally. Add ale and chicken stock and bring to a boil. Add rice with saffron water. Return to boil, stir, cover, and reduce heat to low. Simmer for 20 minutes, stirring every few minutes. Remove from heat and stir in lime juice, salt, and pepper. Let sit uncovered for 5–10 minutes before serving.

Serves 4–6

baked penne with ricotta & pesto

see variations page 68

This delicious pasta casserole is easy to assemble ahead of time. You can pop it in the oven for a hungry crowd and enjoy the compliments, or divide among several smaller dishes and serve in individual portions if you prefer.

1 lb. uncooked penne
1 tbsp. extra-virgin olive oil
1 cup finely chopped yellow onion
2 cloves garlic, minced
1 (28-oz.) can whole tomatoes with liquid

1 tsp. dried oregano
salt and freshly ground black pepper to taste
1 cup ricotta cheese
1/4 cup prepared pesto
2 cups grated mozzarella

Preheat oven to 350°F. In a large pot of salted, boiling water, cook the penne for 7 minutes. The pasta should be barely al dente, as it will continue to cook in the oven. In a large saucepan, heat olive oil over medium heat. Cook onions and garlic until onions are soft and translucent, about 5 minutes. Add undrained tomatoes, oregano, salt, and pepper, using a wooden spoon to break up the tomatoes. Simmer for 10 minutes. In a small bowl, combine ricotta and pesto. Add cooked penne to the tomato sauce. Stir in 1 1/2 cups grated mozzarella. Pour half the pasta into a large casserole, or divide among several smaller ones. Place spoonfuls of the ricotta mixture over the pasta. Pour remaining pasta over the ricotta mixture, and top with remaining 1/2 cup of grated mozzarella. Bake for 20–25 minutes, until casserole is lightly browned and bubbly.

To prepare casserole with ricotta topping, simply place all the pasta mixture in the casserole dish and spread ricotta mixture on top. Sprinkle remaining mozzarella on top and bake for 20–25 minutes, until lightly browned and bubbly.

Serves 4-6

basmati casserole with vidalia onions & emmental cheese

see variations page 69

This rich rice casserole makes a wonderful side dish for roasted chicken or fish.

1/2 cup uncooked basmati rice
8 cups Vidalia onion rings, separated
    (about 3 or 4 onions)
1/2 cup chicken stock

1 1/2 cups grated Emmental cheese
1/4 cup whole milk
salt and freshly ground black pepper to taste
1/4 cup finely chopped Italian parsley

Preheat oven to 350°F. Lightly butter a large casserole.

In a large pot, bring rice to boil in 4 cups of salted water. Boil for 5 minutes, then drain. Transfer rice to casserole, and add all remaining ingredients except parsley. Stir to combine. Cover casserole with aluminum foil and bake for 1 hour, until rice and onions are tender. Remove foil 10 minutes before the end of cooking to brown top of casserole. Sprinkle with parsley before serving.

Serves 4–6

lasagna bolognese

see variations page 70

A foolproof recipe for a perennial favorite, this lasagna can be made up to 24 hours before baking. Simply cover and refrigerate until ready to use.

1 lb. lean ground beef
1/2 cup finely chopped onion
1 clove garlic, minced
1 (16-oz.) can whole tomatoes with liquid
1 (15-oz.) can plain tomato sauce
4 tbsp. finely chopped Italian parsley
4–5 fresh basil leaves, roughly torn

salt and pepper to taste
2 cups ricotta cheese
1/3 cup freshly grated Parmesan, plus 1/4 cup
1 tbsp. finely chopped fresh oregano
pinch of nutmeg
12 lasagna noodles
2 cups grated mozzarella

To prepare the sauce, brown ground beef, onion, and garlic in large, heavy frying pan over medium heat. Cook, stirring occasionally, until beef is brown through; drain. Add tomatoes and tomato sauce, breaking up tomatoes into smaller pieces. Bring to a boil, then reduce heat to low and simmer for 45 minutes, until mixture thickens. Add 2 tablespoons parsley, basil, salt, and pepper. In small bowl, combine ricotta, 1/3 cup Parmesan, remaining 2 tablespoons parsley, oregano, and nutmeg. Preheat oven to 350°F. Cook lasagna noodles in batches in large pot of boiling salted water until al dente, about 9 minutes. Drain and set aside. Distribute 1/2 cup meat sauce over the bottom of a large (9x13-inch) rectangular casserole. Arrange 4 noodles over sauce. Spread another thin layer of sauce (1/2 cup) over noodles. Spoon 1 cup ricotta mixture evenly over sauce. Spread 2/3 cup mozzarella over ricotta. Repeat layers once more, then layer remaining noodles, meat sauce, mozzarella, and Parmesan. Cover lasagna with aluminum foil and bake for 30 minutes. Remove foil and continue baking an additional 15 minutes, until lasagna is heated through and bubbly. Transfer to wire rack and let stand for 10 minutes before serving.

Serves 6–8

kedgeree

see variations page 71

There are many variations of this Indian dish, but most contain some combination of fish, rice, and hard-boiled eggs.

1 1/2 lb. smoked haddock fillets
1/2 cup unsalted butter
1 medium yellow onion, chopped
3/4 tsp. Madras curry powder
1 cup uncooked basmati rice

3 eggs, hard-boiled and chopped
3 tbsp. finely chopped fresh cilantro
1 tbsp. fresh lime juice
salt and freshly ground black pepper to taste

In large saucepan, cover haddock fillets with 2 cups water. Bring to a boil, reduce heat to low, cover, and simmer for 8 minutes. Transfer haddock to a separate dish and cover with aluminum foil. Reserve cooking liquid in large measuring cup.

In same saucepan, melt 1/4 cup butter. Add onion and sauté until onion is translucent, about 5 minutes. Stir in curry powder. Add rice and reserved liquid (2 cups). Stir again, cover, and simmer over low heat for 15 minutes, until rice is tender. Meanwhile, remove skin from haddock and flake with a fork.

When rice is tender, remove from heat and stir in flaked haddock, chopped eggs, cilantro, lime juice, and remaining 1/4 cup butter. Cover saucepan loosely, return to very low heat (if using an electric stove, simply return to hot stovetop but leave burner off), and let sit for 5 minutes. Remove from heat, fluff with fork, and season with salt and pepper.

Serves 4

baked cannelloni

see variations page 72

This versatile Italian casserole can be made with a large variety of fillings, and can be baked in individual portion-sized dishes if you prefer. This is the classic version, but don't miss the exquisite seafood variations.

1 lb. lean ground beef
1 garlic clove, minced
1 cup ricotta cheese
1 cup freshly grated Parmesan
1 egg
1 tsp. dried basil (or 3 tbsp. chopped
    fresh basil)

pinch of freshly grated nutmeg
salt and freshly ground black pepper to taste
12 cannelloni shells
2 1/2 tbsp. unsalted butter
1/4 cup all-purpose flour
2 cups whole milk

Preheat oven to 350°F. To prepare the filling, cook ground beef and garlic in heavy frying pan over medium heat until beef is fully browned, about 7 minutes. Drain and transfer to medium bowl. Add ricotta, 1/2 cup Parmesan, egg, basil, nutmeg, salt, and pepper. Stir to combine and set aside. Bring large pot of salted water to a boil. Add pasta and cook until al dente, about 8 minutes. Drain. To prepare the sauce, melt butter in medium saucepan over low heat. Add flour and stir to make a smooth paste. Cook for 2 minutes. Remove from heat and add milk. Return to medium heat and cook, whisking constantly, until mixture thickens, about 10 minutes. Remove from heat and add nutmeg, salt, and pepper. Stuff the cannelloni with beef and cheese mixture and arrange in buttered large rectangular (9x13-inch) casserole. Pour sauce on top and sprinkle with remaining 1/2 cup Parmesan. Bake for 20–25 minutes, until heated through and golden brown on top.

Serves 4–6

vegetable pastitsio

see variations page 73

This is a vegetarian version of a flavorful Greek layered casserole. Serve with a tossed salad and crusty bread.

8 oz. uncooked shell-shaped pasta
4 tbsp. extra-virgin olive oil
2 garlic cloves, minced
1 (28-oz.) can whole tomatoes in liquid
2 oz. tomato paste
salt and freshly ground black pepper to taste
4 fresh basil leaves, roughly torn

1 tsp. finely chopped fresh oregano
1 tsp. finely chopped fresh thyme
1/2 cup finely sliced onion
1 cup small-cubed eggplant
1 cup small-cubed zucchini
2 eggs, lightly beaten
1/2 cup plain yogurt

Preheat oven to 350°F. Butter a medium casserole. In large pot of salted boiling water, cook pasta until al dente, about 8 minutes. Drain and set aside. Heat 2 tablespoons olive oil in large saucepan over medium heat. Fry garlic until golden, about 4 minutes. Add tomatoes and tomato paste, breaking up tomatoes into smaller pieces, and stirring until tomato paste is well incorporated. Season with salt and pepper and stir in basil, oregano, and thyme. Reduce heat to low and simmer for 10 minutes. In a separate pan, heat remaining oil over medium-high heat and sauté onion, eggplant, and zucchini for 5 minutes, until tender. Season with salt and pepper. In a small bowl, combine eggs and yogurt. Spread half the tomato sauce in casserole. Arrange eggplant–zucchini mixture on top, then top with remaining tomato sauce. Layer pasta over tomato sauce, and spoon yogurt–egg mixture over pasta. Bake for 45 minutes, until yogurt topping is browned and casserole is bubbly.

Serves 4–6

variations

red rice & beef

see base recipe page 46

red rice & beef with beans
Prepare the basic recipe, adding 1 can black beans, rinsed and drained, with the tomatoes.

red rice & beef with feta & olives
Prepare the basic recipe, adding 1/2 cup sliced black olives with the tomatoes. Replace the cheddar cheese with crumbled feta.

rice & beef with mixed peppers
Prepare the basic recipe, reducing the amount of red pepper to 1/4 cup. Add 1/4 cup chopped green bell peppers and 1/4 cup yellow bell peppers.

spicy red rice & beef
Prepare the basic recipe, adding 1/4 teaspoon cayenne, 1/2 teaspoon ground cumin, and 1 teaspoon chili powder with the tomatoes.

red rice & beef with corn & monterey jack
Prepare the basic recipe, adding 1 can corn kernels, rinsed and drained, with the tomatoes. Replace the grated cheddar with an equal quantity of grated Monterey Jack.

rigatoni & italian sausage bake

see base recipe page 46

spicy rigatoni & italian sausage bake
Prepare the basic recipe, replacing the mild Italian sausage with hot Italian sausage.
Add 1/4 teaspoon hot pepper flakes to the sauce with the herbs.

rigatoni & italian sausage bake with roasted red peppers
Prepare the basic recipe, adding 1 (12-ounce) jar roasted red bell peppers, drained
and sliced, when combining the pasta and sauce.

rigatoni & italian sausage bake with fontina
Prepare the basic recipe, substituting grated Fontina for the provolone.

rigatoni & italian sausage bake with mushrooms
Prepare the basic recipe, adding 1 cup chopped cremini mushrooms with the onions
and garlic.

rigatoni & eggplant bake with mozzarella
Prepare the basic recipe, omitting Italian sausage. Toss 2 pounds eggplant, cubed,
with 2 teaspoons salt. Let drain in colander for 30 minutes. Rinse and pat dry.
Heat 1/2 cup extra-virgin olive oil in a Dutch oven. Fry eggplant in batches until
browned, about 5 minutes. Drain eggplant on paper towels, and discard all but
2 tablespoons oil from the pan. Make sauce, adding eggplant 5 minutes before end.
Finish casserole, substituting grated mozzarella for grated provolone.

variations

three cheese & spinach baked manicotti

see base recipe page 49

three cheese & italian parsley baked manicotti

Prepare the basic recipe, omitting spinach. Add 1/4 cup freshly chopped Italian parsley to the cheese mixture.

three cheese & oregano baked manicotti

Prepare the basic recipe, omitting spinach. Add 1 tablespoon freshly chopped oregano to the cheese mixture.

three cheese baked manicotti with meat sauce

Prepare the basic recipe, replacing marinara sauce with a meat sauce. To prepare the sauce, brown 1 pound lean ground beef and 1 cup finely chopped onion in a large, heavy-based frying pan, about 10 minutes. Drain. Add tomatoes and proceed with recipe.

three cheese baked manicotti with mozzarella

Prepare the basic recipe, replacing the cottage cheese with an equal quantity of grated mozzarella.

three cheese baked manicotti with mushroom sauce

Prepare the basic recipe, adding 1 cup sliced cremini mushrooms with the garlic when making the tomato sauce.

variations

arroz con pollo

see base recipe page 50

arroz con pollo with smoked paprika
Prepare the basic recipe, replacing the Spanish paprika in the saffron water
with 1 teaspoon smoked paprika.

arroz con pollo with pimientos
Prepare the basic recipe, garnishing each serving with 2 tablespoons sliced
jarred pimientos.

arroz con pollo with olives
Prepare the basic recipe, garnish each serving with 2 tablespoons chopped
pimiento-stuffed olives.

arroz con pollo with annatto powder
Prepare the basic recipe, replacing the Spanish paprika in the saffron water
with 1 teaspoon annatto powder (sold in Latin American specialty shops).

arroz con pollo with fresh cilantro
Prepare the basic recipe, garnishing each serving with 2 tablespoons freshly
chopped cilantro.

variations

baked penne with ricotta & pesto

see base recipe page 53

baked penne with smooth sauce
Prepare the basic recipe, but allow the sauce to cool to room temperature and purée with an immersion blender before mixing with the penne.

baked penne with mushrooms, ricotta & tapenade
Prepare the basic recipe, adding 1/2 cup sliced mushrooms to sauté with the onions and garlic, and replacing the pesto with tapenade.

baked penne with ricotta and sun-dried tomato pesto
Prepare the basic recipe, replacing the pesto with an equal quantity of sun-dried tomato pesto.

baked penne with ricotta & roasted red peppers
Prepare the basic recipe, adding 1/2 cup sliced roasted red bell peppers to the tomato sauce with the penne and the mozzarella.

baked rigatoni with cottage cheese & pesto
Prepare the basic recipe, replacing the penne with rigatoni and the ricotta with cottage cheese.

basmati casserole with vidalia onions & emmental cheese

see base recipe page 54

jasmine casserole with walla walla onions & emmental

Prepare the basic recipe, substituting jasmine rice for the basmati rice and Walla Walla onions for the Vidalia onions.

basmati casserole with vidalia onions, mushrooms & gruyère

Prepare the basic recipe, adding 1 cup sliced cremini mushrooms to the casserole and substituting Gruyère cheese for the Emmental.

basmati casserole with mixed onions & emmental

Prepare the basic recipe, replacing the Vidalia onions with 3 cups sliced yellow onions, 3 cups sliced red onions, and 2 cups sliced shallots.

basmati casserole with vidalia onions, emmental & sunflower seeds

Prepare the basic recipe, sprinkling 1/2 cup chopped sunflower seeds over casserole before covering and baking.

variations

lasagna bolognese

see base recipe page 57

lighter lasagna bolognese
Prepare the basic recipe, substituting extra-lean ground beef for the lean ground beef; low-fat small curd cottage cheese for the ricotta; and skim-milk mozzarella for the mozzarella.

quick lasagna bolognese
Prepare the basic recipe, omitting the first 7 ingredients. Use 5 cups prepared meat sauce and replace regular lasagna noodles with oven-ready noodles, which do not need to be cooked first.

italian sausage lasagna
Prepare the basic recipe, replacing the lean ground beef with an equal quantity of mild Italian sausage, removed from its casings in small chunks.

vegetarian lasagna
Prepare the basic recipe, omitting the ground beef. Sauté onions and garlic in 2 tablespoons extra-virgin olive oil. Add 1/2 cup peeled and chopped carrot and 1/4 cup chopped celery with the onion and garlic. Add 2 cups chopped fresh spinach and 1 lightly beaten egg to the ricotta mixture.

variations

kedgeree

see base recipe page 58

kedgeree with mango
Prepare the basic recipe, garnishing each serving with 2 slices of fresh mango and 2 tablespoons prepared mango chutney.

kedgeree with yogurt
Prepare the basic recipe, omitting the cilantro. Add 3 tablespoons chopped cilantro to 1 cup plain yogurt and garnish each serving with 1/4 cup of this yogurt mixture.

kedgeree with smoked trout
Prepare the basic recipe, replacing the smoked haddock with an equal quantity of smoked trout fillet.

kedgeree with salmon
Prepare the basic recipe, replacing the smoked haddock with an equal quantity of fresh poached salmon. Cook the salmon in 2 cups of water, but boil for just 3–5 minutes, depending on thickness of fillets. Check fish by flaking the thickest part of the fillet. If it is opaque, salmon is done.

variations

baked cannelloni

see base recipe page 61

baked cannelloni with crab filling
Prepare the basic recipe, replacing ground beef with 1 pound crabmeat. Omit the garlic.

baked cannelloni with spinach filling
Prepare the basic recipe, replacing ground beef and garlic with 2 cups chopped fresh spinach.

baked cannelloni with shrimp filling
Prepare the basic recipe, replacing ground beef and garlic with 1 pound cooked, shelled, deveined, and chopped shrimp.

baked cannelloni with prosciutto filling
Prepare the basic recipe, replacing ground beef and garlic with 1/4 pound chopped prosciutto.

vegetable pastitsio

see base recipe page 62

pastitsio with ground lamb
Prepare the basic recipe, adding 1 pound ground lamb to the tomato sauce.
Brown lamb with the garlic. Drain and proceed with recipe.

pastitsio with ground beef
Prepare the basic recipe, adding 1 pound lean ground beef to the tomato
sauce. Brown beef with the garlic, drain, and proceed with recipe.

pastitsio with macaroni
Prepare the basic recipe, replacing the shell-shaped pasta with an equal
quantity of macaroni.

pastitsio with béchamel
Prepare the basic recipe, replacing the yogurt–egg topping with 2/3 cup
béchamel sauce. To prepare sauce, melt 1 tablespoon butter over medium
heat in small saucepan. Add 1 tablespoon all-purpose flour and stir to form
a smooth paste. When paste starts to boil, remove from heat. Whisk in 1 cup
whole milk. Return to heat and bring to boil, stirring constantly. When sauce
reaches a boil, continue cooking for 2–3 minutes, until mixture thickens.
Remove from heat and add a pinch of salt and a pinch of nutmeg. Spoon
onto pasta and bake as directed.

elegant fare

Casseroles are versatile enough to take on a little elegance when required. So go ahead and make one for your next dinner party — you'll be able to spend more time with your guests and less time in the kitchen. Rustic classics take on an air of sophistication when using the finest ingredients.

pretty paella

see variations page 91

This dish takes the hard work out of the authentic paella. Rather than using a specialty paellera pan over hot coals, this version is cooked in a Dutch oven on the stovetop with equally delightful results.

3 tbsp. extra-virgin olive oil
1 tbsp. finely chopped onion
1/4 tsp. powdered turmeric
1/4 tsp. Spanish paprika
pinch of saffron
1 cup peeled and deveined shrimp
1 cup medium-sized scallops
1 tomato, chopped

1 garlic clove, minced
2 cups prepared fish stock
1 cup medium-grain white rice
6 mussels, in shell
1 red bell pepper, seeded and julienned
salt and freshly ground pepper
1/4 cup finely chopped Italian parsley, to
    garnish

Heat olive oil in a Dutch oven over medium heat. Add onion and sauté until translucent, about 4 minutes. Add turmeric, paprika, and saffron and continue cooking for 1 minute. Add shrimp, scallops, tomato, and garlic. Cook for 5 minutes, stirring occasionally. Raise heat to high, add fish stock, and bring to a boil. Add rice, stir, and reduce heat to low. Cover and cook for 15 minutes. Stir, place mussels and red bell pepper on top of the rice, and cook for another 5–10 minutes, until mussels have opened and pepper is crisp-tender. Discard any unopened mussels. Let sit, uncovered, for 2 minutes. Season to taste. Serve garnished with chopped parsley.

Serves 2

osso bucco

see variations page 92

This wonderful Italian casserole takes its name from the marrowbone. Ask your butcher for large, meaty, crosscut veal shanks for this dish.

4 large (10-oz.) veal shanks
1/4–1/2 cup all-purpose flour
2 tbsp. unsalted butter
1 tbsp. extra-virgin olive oil
1/2 large onion, finely chopped
1 celery rib, diced
1 carrot, diced
1/2 cup white wine
1 3/4 cups canned whole tomatoes with liquid

2 garlic cloves, minced
1 tbsp. finely chopped Italian parsley, plus
    1/4 cup, to garnish
1/4 tsp. dried summer savory
1/4 tsp. dried rosemary, crushed
1 1/2 cups low-sodium chicken stock
salt and freshly ground black pepper to taste
zest of 1/2 lemon, to garnish

Preheat oven to 325°F. Lightly coat veal shanks in flour. Heat 1 tablespoon butter and the oil in Dutch oven and brown veal on all sides, about 10–12 minutes. Transfer veal to plate and set aside. Melt remaining butter in Dutch oven. Sauté onions, celery, and carrots until onions are translucent and celery and carrots are tender, about 5 minutes. Add white wine and cook, letting some of the liquid evaporate. Add tomatoes, garlic, 1 tablespoon parsley, summer savory, rosemary, and 1 cup chicken stock. Raise heat and bring to a boil. Arrange veal shanks in a single layer in the sauce, then reduce to simmer. Cover Dutch oven and transfer to oven. Braise for 2–2 1/2 hours, until meat is very tender and falling off the bone. Check after 1 1/2 hours and, if necessary, add up to 1/2 cup more chicken stock. Season to taste. Sprinkle each serving with the 1/4 cup chopped parsley and lemon zest.

Serves 4

coq au vin

see variations page 93

This one is always a crowd-pleaser. Serve with a tossed salad and a crusty loaf of French bread — perfect for soaking up any leftover juices.

1/2 cup all-purpose flour
1 1/2 tsp. salt
1/4 tsp. freshly ground black pepper
1 (3–3 1/2-lb.) whole chicken, cut into 8 pieces
6 slices thick-sliced bacon
6 whole pearl onions, peeled
2 cloves garlic, minced
1/2 cup roughly chopped celery

1 cup roughly chopped carrot
1 cup sliced cremini mushrooms
1 cup low-sodium chicken stock
1 cup dry white wine
1/2 tsp. dried thyme
1 bay leaf
2 tbsp. finely chopped Italian parsley

In a small bowl, combine flour with 1 teaspoon salt and the pepper. Clean chicken and pat dry with paper towel. Coat chicken pieces evenly with seasoned flour. Set aside. In a large Dutch oven or heavy-based saucepan with lid, fry bacon over medium-high heat until crisp. Transfer to a plate covered with a paper towel to drain.

Brown chicken on all sides in bacon fat. Add onions, garlic, celery, carrot, and mushrooms, stirring until onions are tender, 8–10 minutes. Drain fat from Dutch oven. Crumble bacon and add to chicken and vegetables. Add chicken stock, wine, remaining 1/2 teaspoon salt, thyme, bay leaf, and parsley. Reduce heat to low, place cover on Dutch oven, and simmer for 1 hour, or until chicken is tender. Remove bay leaf before serving.

Serves 4

boeuf bourguignon

see variations page 94

Rich and succulent, this classic French casserole takes on the flavor of the red wine you choose, so make it a good one!

4 thick slices bacon
3 lb. stewing beef, cut into 1-inch cubes
salt and freshly ground black pepper to taste
1/3 cup all-purpose flour
4 medium-sized onions, sliced
2 cloves garlic, minced
1 lb. cremini mushrooms, sliced

1 tbsp. tomato paste
3 cups prepared beef stock
3 1/2 cups red wine (such as a Burgundy)
1/2 of 1 celery rib
4 fresh parsley stems
4 fresh thyme sprigs
2 bay leaves

In a large Dutch oven or heavy-based saucepan with lid, fry bacon until crisp over medium-high heat. Transfer to a plate covered with a paper towel to drain. Pat beef dry with paper towel, then season with salt and pepper. Coat evenly with flour. Brown beef all over in bacon fat. Transfer to separate bowl. Add onions, garlic, and mushrooms to the Dutch oven and sauté until onions are translucent, about 5 minutes. Transfer onions and mushrooms to separate dish. Add tomato paste to Dutch oven and cook for 1 minute, stirring.

Crumble bacon. Return bacon and beef to Dutch oven. Add beef stock and red wine. Make a bouquet garni by tying celery, parsley, thyme, and bay leaves together with kitchen string. Add to beef mixture and simmer for 3 1/2-4 hours, until meat is tender. Return onions, garlic, and mushrooms to Dutch oven and cook for 10 minutes. Remove bouquet garni, skim any fat from surface of pan, and serve.

Serves 6-8

rabbit braised in white wine

see variations page 95

If you have never prepared rabbit at home before, this uncomplicated recipe with impressive results is the perfect place to start. Have your butcher cut the rabbit for you.

1/2 cup all-purpose flour
salt
1/4 tsp. freshly ground black pepper
1 (3-lb.) rabbit, cut into 6 pieces
2 tbsp. extra-virgin olive oil
1/2 lb. whole shallots, peeled

4 garlic cloves, peeled
1 lb. new potatoes
1 bottle dry white wine
2 bay leaves
2 tbsp. chopped fresh chives, to garnish

In a small bowl, combine flour with 1/2 teaspoon salt and 1/4 teaspoon pepper. Clean rabbit and pat dry with paper towel, then coat pieces evenly with seasoned flour. Set aside.

In a large Dutch oven, heat oil over medium-high heat. Brown rabbit pieces for 5 minutes per side. Transfer to plate and set aside. Reduce heat to medium. Add shallots to Dutch oven, sprinkle with salt, and sauté until translucent, about 5 minutes. Add garlic and cook for 3 more minutes. Add potatoes and rabbit pieces to Dutch oven. Pour in wine, stir, and add bay leaves. Bring to a boil, then reduce heat to low. Cover Dutch oven and simmer for up to 3 hours, until rabbit is tender and still moist. Remove bay leaves. Serve garnished with chopped chives.

Serves 4

lobster florentine

see variations page 96

This easy casserole will be met with "oohs" and "aahs." Serve as an elegant side dish, or as an appetizer with thin slices of toasted baguette.

1 lb. cooked lobster meat, cut into bite-sized
    pieces
3 tbsp. unsalted butter
2 tbsp. all-purpose flour
1 cup heavy cream
1/2 cup freshly grated Parmesan
1/4 cup dry breadcrumbs

1 tbsp. Chesapeake seasoning blend (such as
    Old Bay)
salt and freshly ground black pepper to taste
1 (10-oz.) package frozen spinach, thawed and
    drained
1 cup grated mozzarella

Preheat oven to 350°F. Butter a 9-inch pie plate, then arrange lobster meat in a layer on the bottom. In medium saucepan, melt butter over medium heat. Add flour and stir constantly, until mixture is smooth and bubbling. Continue stirring for 1 minute, then remove from heat. Whisk in cream and return to stove. Bring mixture to boil, whisking constantly. When mixture has thickened, about 1–2 minutes after it comes to a boil, add 1/4 cup Parmesan. Stir until blended and remove from heat.

In small bowl, combine breadcrumbs with Chesapeake seasoning, salt, and pepper. Set aside. Place paper towel in a fine sieve and press spinach lightly to remove any remaining liquid. Spread spinach over lobster in pie plate. Pour cream sauce over spinach. Sprinkle mozzarella cheese on top, then sprinkle with remaining 1/4 cup Parmesan and the breadcrumb mixture. Bake for 20 minutes, or until casserole is heated through and is brown and bubbly.

Serves 4–6 as a side dish

shrimp & wild rice casserole

see variations page 97

A mouthwatering concoction that will leave guests asking for more.

1 cup wild rice
1/2 tsp. salt, plus extra to taste
1 lb. medium shrimp, peeled and deveined
1/4 cup unsalted butter, plus 2 tbsp.
1/2 cup finely chopped onion

1/2 cup seeded and diced yellow bell pepper
1/4 cup all-purpose flour
1/4 tsp. freshly ground pepper
2 cups whole milk
2 cups grated sharp white cheddar

Preheat oven to 325°F. Butter a medium casserole. Cook the rice according to package directions, reducing water by 1/4 cup. Drain and set aside. In a medium saucepan, bring 2 cups water and 1/2 teaspoon salt to boil. Cook shrimp for 1 minute. Drain and set aside. Melt 2 tablespoons butter in saucepan and sauté onion and bell pepper until onion is translucent, about 5 minutes. Set aside.

In large saucepan, melt remaining 1/4 cup butter over medium heat. Add flour, salt to taste, and the pepper. Stir constantly, until mixture is smooth and bubbling. Continue stirring for 1 minute, then remove from heat. Whisk in milk, then return to stove. Bring mixture to a boil, whisking continuously. When mixture has thickened, about 1–2 minutes after it comes to a boil, add 1 1/2 cups of the cheese. Stir until blended and remove from heat. Stir in rice, shrimp, onion, and pepper. Pour mixture into prepared casserole dish and top with remaining cheese. Bake for 30 minutes, until bubbly.

Serves 6–8

risotto with pancetta & parmesan

see variations page 98

Creamy rice, salty pancetta, and fragrant basil blend beautifully in this understated yet refined dish.

1 tbsp. unsalted butter
1 tbsp. extra-virgin olive oil
1/2 cup finely chopped onion
1 garlic clove, minced
1/2 cup roughly chopped thin-sliced pancetta
1 1/3 cups Arborio rice

3/4 cup dry white wine
4 cups low-sodium chicken stock
salt and freshly ground black pepper to taste
3/4 cup freshly grated Parmesan
6 fresh basil leaves, torn, to garnish

In a Dutch oven over medium heat, heat butter and oil together. Add onion, garlic, and pancetta. Sauté, stirring constantly, until onion is translucent, about 5 minutes. Add rice and stir until butter and oil have been absorbed. Remove Dutch oven from heat and add wine and 1 cup chicken stock. Return to stovetop over low heat and simmer for 10–15 minutes, stirring frequently. When liquid is almost all absorbed, add another cup of stock. Continue stirring and adding stock in this manner until all the stock is incorporated, the rice is tender, and the mixture is creamy. Remove from heat, season with salt and pepper, and stir in 1/2 cup Parmesan. Serve garnished with torn basil leaves and remaining Parmesan.

Serves 2 as a main course, 3–4 as a side dish

lamb navarin

see variations page 99

This recipe will achieve best results when made with fresh spring lamb. Serve with boiled new potatoes tossed with parsley and butter.

2 lb. boneless leg of lamb, cut into
    2-inch cubes
salt and freshly ground black pepper to taste
3 tbsp. all-purpose flour
2 tbsp. extra-virgin olive oil
1 tsp. granulated sugar

1 large yellow onion, cut into 8 segments
1 garlic clove, minced
4 carrots, roughly chopped
1 cup low-sodium chicken stock
1 sprig of thyme

Pat lamb dry with paper towel and season with salt and pepper. Coat evenly with flour. Heat oil in large saucepan over medium-high heat. Brown lamb, cooking for about 4 minutes per side and sprinkling with a pinch of sugar before turning pieces to help crust caramelize in places. Transfer lamb to bowl. Add onion, garlic, and carrots to saucepan. Cook until onions begin to soften, about 3 minutes. Return lamb to saucepan. Add chicken stock and thyme. Bring to a boil, cover saucepan, and reduce heat to medium-low. Simmer for 1–1 1/2 hours, until lamb is tender. Skim any fat from surface of pan, transfer to serving dish, and serve.

Serves 4

pretty paella

see base recipe page 75

pretty paella with squid
Prepare the basic recipe, replacing the scallops with squid.

pretty paella with chicken
Prepare the basic recipe, replacing the scallops with 1/2 pound skinless, boneless chicken thighs, cubed.

pretty paella with artichokes
Prepare the basic recipe, adding 1 can artichoke hearts, drained and roughly chopped, before adding the mussels.

pretty paella with peas
Prepare the basic recipe, adding 1 cup peas before adding the mussels.

pretty paella with clams
Prepare the basic recipe, replacing the shrimp with an equal quantity of small, hard-shelled clams.

variations

osso bucco

see base recipe page 76

osso bucco with olives
Prepare the basic recipe, adding 1/2 cup pitted and halved kalamata olives with the tomatoes.

osso bucco with cremini mushrooms
Prepare the basic recipe, stirring in 1 cup sautéed cremini mushrooms before serving. To prepare mushrooms, melt 1 tablespoon unsalted butter in frying pan. Sauté quartered mushrooms, sprinkled with salt, pepper, and a pinch of thyme. Cook until mushrooms begin to give off liquid. Remove from heat.

osso bucco with gremolata
Prepare the basic recipe, omitting lemon–parsley garnish. To make gremolata, combine 2 tablespoons chopped parsley, 2 tablespoons minced garlic, and 1 tablespoon grated lemon zest. Garnish each serving with gremolata.

osso bucco with peppers
Prepare the basic recipe, adding 1/2 cup chopped red bell pepper with the carrot and celery.

osso bucco with red wine
Prepare the basic recipe, replacing the white wine with red wine.

variations

coq au vin

see base recipe page 79

coq au vin rouge
Prepare the basic recipe, replacing the white wine with an equal quantity
of red wine.

coq au vin with cipollini onions
Prepare the basic recipe, replacing pearl onions with 6–8 whole cipollini
onions, trimmed and peeled.

coq au vin with morels
Prepare the basic recipe, replacing the cremini mushrooms with an equal
quantity of morels. If you cannot get fresh morels, use dried morels, taking
the time to rehydrate and clean them thoroughly before using.

coq au champagne
Prepare the basic recipe, replacing the white wine with an equal quantity of
champagne.

coq au vin with brandy
Prepare the basic recipe, adding 1/3 cup brandy after browning the chicken.

variations

boeuf bourguignon

see base recipe page 80

boeuf bourguignon with parsnips
Prepare the basic recipe, adding 2 parsnips, peeled and roughly chopped, with the carrots.

boeuf bourguignon with portobellos
Prepare the basic recipe, replacing cremini mushrooms with an equal quantity of portobellos, cleaned and roughly chopped.

boeuf bourguignon with pancetta
Prepare the basic recipe, replacing the bacon with 8 ounces cubed pancetta.

bison bourguignon
Prepare the basic recipe, replacing the stewing beef with an equal quantity of bison meat.

boeuf bourguignon with peas
Prepare the basic recipe, adding 1/2 cup fresh or frozen peas when returning onions and mushrooms to Dutch oven.

variations

rabbit braised in white wine

see base recipe page 83

rabbit braised in red wine
Prepare the basic recipe, replacing the white wine with an equal quantity of red wine.

rabbit braised in champagne
Prepare the basic recipe, replacing the white wine with an equal quantity of champagne or sparkling wine.

rabbit braised in white wine with dill
Prepare the basic recipe, replacing the chopped chives with an equal quantity of freshly chopped dill.

chicken braised in white wine
Prepare the basic recipe, replacing the rabbit with 1 (3-pound) broiler chicken, cut into 8 pieces.

rabbit braised in white wine with pesto
Prepare the basic recipe, replacing the chopped chives with 1 teaspoon prepared pesto per serving.

variations

lobster florentine

see base recipe page 84

crab florentine
Prepare the basic recipe, replacing the lobster meat with crabmeat.

scallop florentine
Prepare the basic recipe, replacing the lobster meat with 1 pound sea scallops. To prepare the scallops, simply bring a large pot of water to a boil. Immerse scallops and boil for 2 minutes. Remove scallops with a slotted spoon and pat dry with paper towel.

lobster florentine with fresh basil
Prepare the basic recipe, adding 2 tablespoons freshly chopped basil to the Chesapeake seasoning and breadcrumbs before sprinkling over the sauce.

lobster florentine with italian parsley
Prepare the basic recipe, adding 1/4 cup freshly chopped Italian parsley to the Chesapeake seasoning and breadcrumbs before sprinkling over cheese sauce.

shrimp & wild rice casserole

see base recipe page 87

shrimp & brown rice casserole
Prepare the basic recipe, replacing the wild rice with an equal quantity of brown rice. Prepare brown rice according to package directions.

shrimp & wild rice casserole with broccoli
Prepare the basic recipe, adding 1 cup steamed broccoli florets when combining shrimp and rice. To steam broccoli, place florets in steamer in saucepan with 1 inch water. Bring water to boil over medium-high heat, and steam broccoli for 3–5 minutes, until crisp-tender.

shrimp & wild rice casserole with asparagus spears
Prepare the basic recipe, adding 1 cup steamed asparagus spears when combining shrimp and rice. To steam asparagus, place spears in steamer in saucepan with 1 inch water. Bring water to boil over medium-high heat, and steam asparagus for 3–4 minutes, until crisp-tender.

shrimp & basmati casserole
Prepare the basic recipe, replacing the wild rice with an equal quantity of basmati rice. Prepare basmati according to package directions.

risotto with pancetta & parmesan

see base recipe page 88

risotto with pancetta, zucchini & parmesan
Prepare the basic recipe, adding 1 cup grated zucchini once the rice has absorbed all the butter and oil. Cook zucchini for 1 minute and proceed with recipe.

risotto with pancetta, wild mushrooms & parmesan
Prepare the basic recipe, adding 1 cup roughly chopped mixed wild mushrooms, once the rice has absorbed the butter and oil. Cook mushrooms for 2–3 minutes, then proceed with recipe.

risotto with pancetta, tomato & parmesan
Prepare the basic recipe, stirring in 1 finely chopped tomato once the rice has absorbed the butter and oil. Cook tomato for 1 minute, then proceed with recipe.

risotto with pancetta, corn & parmesan
Prepare the basic recipe, adding 1/2 cup fresh corn kernels to the risotto after the last addition of chicken stock.

lamb navarin

see base recipe page 90

lamb navarin with rutabaga
Prepare the basic recipe, adding 1 cup peeled and cubed rutabaga with the carrots.

lamb navarin with parsnips
Prepare the basic recipe, adding 2 parsnips, peeled and roughly chopped, with the carrots.

lamb navarin with rosemary
Prepare the basic recipe, replacing sprig of thyme with a sprig of rosemary.

lamb navarin with mint
Prepare the basic recipe, replacing the sprig of thyme with 1 tablespoon freshly chopped mint.

meat casseroles

On nights when you are craving an extra dose of
protein, the casseroles in this chapter are sure to
please. By combining pork, beef, or lamb with other
ingredients, you can include meat in your family's
diet in a healthy and economical way.

braised pork with fennel

see variations page 117

Tender pork and aromatic fennel are a match made in heaven. Serve with a dish of garlic-mashed potatoes.

3 tsp. extra-virgin olive oil
1 medium onion, sliced
1 large fennel bulb, ends trimmed, halved
    and sliced
2 celery ribs, trimmed and diced

2 garlic cloves, minced
1 (28-oz.) can whole tomatoes with liquid
1/2 cup low-sodium chicken stock
4 pork loin cutlets, trimmed of excess fat
2 tsp. finely chopped fresh thyme, to garnish

Preheat oven to 350°F. In large heatproof casserole, heat 2 teaspoons olive oil over medium heat. Add onion, fennel, and celery. Cover and cook, stirring occasionally, for 10 minutes, until vegetables become tender. Add garlic and continue cooking for another minute. Add tomatoes, breaking them up into smaller pieces. Stir in chicken stock and bring to a boil. Remove from heat.

Heat remaining 1 teaspoon oil in large nonstick frying pan over high heat. Add pork cutlets and brown for 2 minutes on each side. Add browned cutlets to fennel mixture in casserole dish. Cover and cook for 1 hour, until pork is tender. Remove from oven and serve, garnished with fresh thyme.

Serves 4

lamb & green bean casserole

see variations page 118

This casserole can be made ahead and reheated on the stovetop. If you prefer your beans crisp-tender, add them in the last 10 minutes of cooking, and return to oven without the lid.

2 tbsp. extra-virgin olive oil
1 lb. lamb, cut into 1-inch cubes
1 cup finely chopped red onions
1 tbsp. unsalted butter
2 garlic cloves, minced

1 1/4 cups canned whole tomatoes with liquid
1/2 tsp. salt
1/4 tsp. dried oregano
2 cups water
3/4 lb. fresh green beens, topped and tailed

Preheat oven to 350°F. Put oil in large Dutch oven over high heat. Add lamb and brown, about 4 minutes per side. Add onions and sauté until they begin to brown, about 6 minutes. Add butter and garlic. Cook for 2 minutes, then add tomatoes. Break tomatoes into smaller pieces. Add salt and oregano. Stir in water and bring to a boil.

Place lid on Dutch oven and transfer to oven. Cook for 1 hour. Remove from oven, add beans and more water if necessary. Return to oven for another 45 minutes. Remove from oven and let sit, covered, for another 30 minutes.

Serves 4

classic stroganoff

see variations page 119

Succulent strips of sirloin in a creamy mushroom sauce make for pure comfort food.

2 tbsp. all-purpose flour
1/2 tsp. salt, plus to taste
1/4 tsp. freshly ground black pepper, plus
    to taste
1 1/2 lb. sirloin steak, sliced into 2-inch strips
2 tbsp. extra-virgin olive oil
4 tbsp. unsalted butter
1/2 cup sliced onion
1 garlic clove, minced

2 cups sliced button mushrooms
1/2 cup sherry
1/2 cup beef broth
1/4 cup finely chopped Italian parsley,
    plus 3 tbsp.
1 tbsp. fresh lemon juice
1/2 tsp. Spanish paprika
1 cup sour cream

In shallow dish, combine flour, 1/2 teaspoon salt, and 1/4 teaspoon pepper. Dredge steak in seasoned flour. In large Dutch oven, heat oil and 2 tablespoons butter over medium heat. Brown steak on both sides and transfer to a plate. Set aside.

Add remaining 2 tablespoons butter to Dutch oven. Sauté onions, garlic, and mushrooms about 3 minutes. Return steak to Dutch oven. Add sherry, beef broth, 3 tablespoons parsley, lemon juice, and paprika. Season with salt and pepper to taste. Simmer for another 5 minutes. Stir in sour cream and continue cooking over medium heat until warmed through. Remove from heat and serve, garnished with remaining parsley.

Serves 6

choucroute garni

see variations page 120

This dish originates from Alsace, a region of northeastern France that borders Germany and Switzerland. You will find influences of all three countries in this tasty casserole.

4 cups prepared sauerkraut, drained
5 tbsp. unsalted butter
6 slices thick-sliced bacon, cubed
1 carrot, diced
1 medium onion, sliced
1 bay leaf
1/2 tsp. dried thyme

1/4 tsp. freshly ground black pepper
1/2 cup dry white wine
2 cups low-sodium chicken stock
4 pork cutlets
salt and freshly ground black pepper to taste
8 German pork sausages

Preheat oven to 325°F. Place drained sauerkraut in large bowl, cover with water, stir, and drain again. In a large Dutch oven over medium heat, melt 3 tablespoons butter. Add bacon, carrot, onion, bay leaf, thyme, and pepper. Cook until onions become translucent, about 5 minutes. Add wine, bring to boil, and let simmer until liquid has reduced by half. Add chicken stock and sauerkraut. Stir and cover Dutch oven with lid. Bring to a boil, then transfer to the preheated oven. Cook for 1 hour.

In a heavy-based frying pan over medium heat, melt remaining 2 tablespoons butter. Add pork cutlets, season with salt and pepper, and sauté until browned, about 6 minutes per side. Add browned cutlets and sausages to Dutch oven, cover, and return to oven for another hour.

Serves 4

beef enchilada casserole

see variations page 121

This authentic Mexican casserole will warm you up on chilly nights. Adjust seasonings to accommodate your own spice preferences.

1 lb. extra-lean ground beef
1 cup finely chopped onion
5 tbsp. chili powder
2 tsp. salt
3/4 tsp. plus a pinch of garlic powder
pinch of ground red pepper
2 1/2 tsp. ground cumin
5 1/2 cups water, plus 6 tbsp.

4 tbsp. canola oil, plus more for frying
8 (6-inch) corn tortillas
6 tbsp. all-purpose flour
1 1/4 cups grated sharp cheddar
1 1/4 cups grated Monterey Jack
sour cream, to garnish
chopped green onion, to garnish

To prepare beef filling, brown beef and onion in a large, heavy-based saucepan over medium heat. Drain off fat, then stir in 2 tablespoons chili powder, 1/2 teaspoon salt, pinch of garlic powder and ground red pepper, and 1 teaspoon cumin. Add 1 cup water, bring to a boil, and reduce heat to low. Cover and simmer for 25 minutes. Set aside.

Fill large, deep frying pan with 1/4 inch canola oil. Once oil is hot, use tongs to dip a tortilla in oil. Fry tortilla for 5 seconds per side. Transfer carefully to plate lined with paper towel to drain. Repeat with remaining tortillas, then set aside.

To prepare enchilada sauce, combine 4 tbsp. canola oil, 3 tablespoons chili powder, flour, remaining 1 1/2 teaspoon cumin, 3/4 teaspoon garlic powder, and 1 1/2 teaspoon salt in medium-sized saucepan over medium heat.

Stir to make a smooth paste, then add 4 1/2 cups water, stirring frequently. Bring to a boil, reduce to simmer, and cook for 4–5 minutes, until mixture thickens slightly. Remove from heat, and let cool for a few minutes.

Preheat oven to 350°F. Butter 9x13x2-inch casserole. In a bowl, combine grated cheeses. Working with one at a time, dip tortilla in enchilada sauce. Allow excess sauce to drip back into saucepan, then transfer tortilla to plate. Place 1/4 cup beef filling in center of tortilla. Top with 1/4 cup grated cheese. Roll tortilla up, and place, seam-side down, in buttered casserole. Repeat with all tortillas. Pour 1 cup enchilada sauce over enchiladas. Bake for 20–25 minutes, until enchiladas are heated through and sauce is bubbly. Remove from oven, top with remaining grated cheese, and serve garnished with sour cream and green onions.

Serves 4

pork tenderloin with mushroom sauce

see variations page 122

Slowly braising pork in red wine adds depth and personality to this beautifully tender meat. You could use individual portion-sized casserole dishes as shown here, if preferred.

1 tbsp. extra-virgin olive oil
1 lb. pork tenderloin, cut into 1-inch cubes
3 slices bacon, roughly chopped
1 garlic clove, minced
1/2 cup finely chopped shallots

1/2 cup sliced cremini mushrooms
1/4 tsp. dried thyme
1 tbsp. finely chopped Italian parsley
1 cup red wine
salt and freshly ground black pepper to taste

Preheat oven to 350°F. Heat oil in large casserole dish over medium-high heat, then add pork. Brown about 4 minutes per side. Add bacon and continue cooking for another 2 minutes. Transfer pork and bacon to a bowl and set aside.

Add garlic and shallots to casserole dish. Sauté until shallots become tender, about 4 minutes. Add mushrooms, thyme, and parsley, and cook for another 4 minutes.

Return pork and bacon to the casserole. Add red wine and stir. If desired, divide the mixture between 2–3 individual portion-sized dishes. Transfer the casserole(s) to the oven and cook for 1 1/2 hours, uncovered. Remove from oven, stir, and add salt and pepper to taste.

Serves 2–3

polenta casserole with italian sausage

see variations page 123

This casserole makes a great lunch offering, served with ratatouille or mixed grilled vegetables.

3 tbsp. unsalted butter
3 oz. pancetta, cut into small cubes
10 oz. mild Italian sausage, casings removed,
    crumbled

7 cups water
1 1/2 cups fine cornmeal
3/4 cup mozzarella, cut into 1/2-inch cubes
1/3 cup freshly grated Parmesan

Preheat oven to 400°F. Butter a 13x9x2-inch casserole or large earthenware dish. In large, heavy-based frying pan, melt 1 tablespoon butter over medium-high heat. Add pancetta and cook until it begins to get crisp, about 3 minutes. Transfer pancetta with drippings to heatproof bowl and set aside. In same frying pan, brown sausage about 8 minutes. Transfer to plate with paper towel to drain.

In large, heavy-based saucepan, bring water to a boil. Add cornmeal, pouring it slowly in a continuous stream, whisking constantly. Reduce heat to low and cook, stirring almost constantly, for 20 minutes or until polenta thickens and pulls away from sides of saucepan. Remove from heat. Stir in pancetta with drippings, cubed mozzarella, and remaining butter. Transfer polenta mixture to buttered casserole or earthenware dish, spread sausage on top, and sprinkle with grated Parmesan. Bake for 25 minutes, or until polenta is set and Parmesan has melted.

Serves 8

long-simmered beef daube

see variations page 124

Something magical happens to beef when it is left for hours to absorb the flavors of stock, wine, vegetables, and herbs. Be forewarned, however; the aroma will have your mouth watering before the casserole is ready to be eaten!

2 tbsp. extra-virgin olive oil
2 garlic cloves, minced
2 lb. stewing beef, cut into 2-inch cubes
1 1/2 tsp. salt
1/2 tsp. freshly ground black pepper
1 cup full red wine, such as a Syrah
2 cups diced carrots
1 1/2 cups finely chopped onions

1/2 cup low-sodium beef broth
1 tbsp. tomato paste
1/4 tsp. dried rosemary, crumbled
1/4 tsp. dried thyme
pinch of ground cloves
1 (14 1/2-oz.) can whole tomatoes with juice
1 bay leaf
4 cups egg noodles

Preheat oven to 300°F. In large Dutch oven, heat olive oil over medium-low heat. Add garlic and cook for 4 minutes. Transfer garlic to small dish and set aside. Raise heat to medium-high and brown beef, seasoned with 1/2 teaspoon salt and 1/4 teaspoon pepper, about 4 minutes per side. Transfer beef to a separate dish and set aside. Add wine to Dutch oven and bring to a boil as you scrape sides and bottom of pot. Return garlic and beef to Dutch oven. Add remaining salt and pepper and all the remaining ingredients except the noodles. Bring to a boil, stir, cover, and transfer to oven for 2 1/2 hours.

Prepare egg noodles according to package directions 10 minutes before removing the casserole from the oven. Remove bay leaf. Serve casserole over noodles.

Serves 4–6

veal parmigiana

see variations page 125

This is a simplified, but no less delicious, version of the classic Italian preparation.

2 tbsp. unsalted butter, melted
1/2 cup freshly grated Parmesan, plus 2 tbsp.
1/4 cup all-purpose flour
1/2 tsp. salt

1/4 tsp. freshly ground black pepper
2/3 cup evaporated milk
4 veal cutlets
8 oz. plain tomato sauce

Preheat oven to 350°F. Pour melted butter into an 8-inch square casserole. In a small bowl, combine 2 tablespoons grated Parmesan, flour, salt, and pepper. Pour 1/3 cup evaporated milk into a shallow dish. Dip each veal cutlet in the milk, coating both sides. Then roll each cutlet in the flour mixture. Place the veal in a single layer in casserole and bake for 30 minutes.

In another bowl, combine remaining 1/3 cup evaporated milk with 1/2 cup Parmesan. Remove veal from oven. Pour tomato sauce around the cutlets, then spread the milk and Parmesan mixture over each cutlet. Return to oven for another 20–25 minutes until bubbly. Veal should be faintly pink in center when sliced.

Serves 4

braised pork with fennel

see base recipe page 101

braised pork with fennel & mint
Prepare the basic recipe, replacing chopped thyme with an equal quantity of freshly chopped mint.

cider braised pork with fennel & apples
Prepare the basic recipe, omitting tomatoes. Add 1 cup apple cider and 1 cup peeled and chopped apple in the place of the tomatoes. Cook for 5 minutes, until apples become tender, then proceed with recipe.

braised pork with fennel & mushrooms
Prepare the basic recipe, adding 1/2 pound quartered white mushrooms with the onion, fennel, and celery.

braised pork with fennel & peppers
Prepare the basic recipe, adding 1/2 cup seeded and chopped green bell pepper with the onion, fennel, and celery.

variations

lamb & green bean casserole

see base recipe page 102

lamb & green bean casserole with feta
Prepare the basic recipe, garnishing each serving with 2 tablespoons
crumbled feta cheese.

lamb & kale casserole
Prepare the basic recipe, replacing the green beans with 2 cups rinsed and
coarsely chopped kale.

lamb & pea casserole
Prepare the basic recipe, omitting green beans. Add 2 cups peas in the last
10 minutes of cooking.

lamb & zucchini casserole
Prepare the basic recipe, omitting green beans. Add 2 cups diced zucchini
with the garlic.

lamb & green bean casserole with potatoes
Prepare the basic recipe, adding 1 pound peeled and cubed potatoes for the
last hour of cooking.

variations

classic stroganoff

see base recipe page 105

lighter stroganoff
Prepare the basic recipe, omitting the butter and replacing the sour cream with 1/2 cup buttermilk. Top each serving with 1 tablespoon of low-fat sour cream.

classic stroganoff with grainy mustard
Prepare the basic recipe, adding 2 tablespoons grainy mustard to the sour cream before adding it to the beef mixture.

chicken stroganoff
Prepare the basic recipe, replacing the sirloin steak with an equal quantity of skinless, boneless chicken breast.

mushroom stroganoff with seitan
Prepare the basic recipe, replacing the ground beef with 2 cups sliced seitan and omitting the flour. Simply season seitan with salt and pepper and proceed with recipe.

classic stroganoff with hot hungarian paprika
Prepare the basic recipe, replacing the Spanish paprika with an equal quantity of hot Hungarian paprika.

variations

choucroute garni

see base recipe page 106

choucroute garni with caraway seeds
Prepare the basic recipe, adding 1 teaspoon caraway seeds with the bay leaf and thyme.

choucroute garni with juniper berries
Prepare the basic recipe, adding 4–6 juniper berries with the bay leaf and thyme.

choucroute garni with riesling
Prepare the basic recipe, replacing the white wine with an equal quantity of Riesling.

choucroute garni with ham
Prepare the basic recipe, adding 1 pound smoked ham to the Dutch oven with the browned pork and sausages.

choucroute garni with new potatoes
Prepare the basic recipe, adding 1 pound halved new potatoes to the Dutch oven with the browned pork and sausages.

beef enchilada casserole

see base recipe page 108

chicken enchilada casserole
Prepare the basic recipe, omitting beef filling. To prepare chicken filling, cook
4 skinless, boneless chicken breasts in a nonstick frying pan over medium heat
until juices run clear, 10–12 minutes. Drain fat from pan, cube chicken, and return
to pan. Add 1 finely chopped onion, 3/4 cup sour cream, 1 cup grated cheddar
cheese, and 1/2 teaspoon dried oregano. Cook over low heat, stirring, until cheese
has melted. Stir in 1 cup salsa and 1 1/2 teaspoons chili powder.

cheese enchilada casserole
Prepare the basic recipe, omitting beef filling. To prepare cheese filling, combine
1 pound grated cheddar cheese, 1 finely chopped medium onion, 1 teaspoon dried
oregano, and 3 tablespoons pitted and chopped black olives.

refried bean enchilada casserole
Prepare the basic recipe, omitting beef filling. To prepare bean filling, combine
2 cups refried beans, 1 cup cottage cheese, and 1 cup grated cheddar cheese.

turkey enchilada casserole
Prepare the basic recipe, replacing the ground beef with ground turkey.

beef enchilada casserole with cilantro
Prepare the basic recipe, garnishing the casserole with 1/4 cup finely chopped fresh
cilantro before serving.

variations

pork tenderloin with mushroom sauce

see base recipe page 110

pork tenderloin with mushroom & white wine sauce
Prepare the basic recipe, replacing the red wine with an equal quantity of white wine.

pork tenderloin with wild mushroom sauce
Prepare the basic recipe, replacing the cremini mushrooms with an equal quantity of mixed wild mushrooms (morels, chanterelles, and porcini).

pork tenderloin with truffle sauce
Prepare the basic recipe, adding 2 teaspoons truffle oil to the fat in the pan before adding the garlic and shallots. Replace red wine with an equal quantity of white wine.

pork tenderloin with mushroom sauce & pappardelle
Prepare the basic recipe, then serve each portion with 1/2 cup cooked pappardelle. Cook pappardelle following package instructions.

polenta casserole with italian sausage

see base recipe page 113

polenta casserole with italian sausage & olives
Prepare the basic recipe, adding 1/2 cup pitted and chopped kalamata olives
when combining the polenta and sausage.

polenta casserole with italian sausage & asiago
Prepare the basic recipe, replacing the mozzarella with an equal quantity of
cubed Asiago cheese.

polenta casserole with italian sausage & roasted red peppers
Prepare the basic recipe, adding 1/2 cup drained and chopped roasted red
bell peppers when combining the polenta and sausage.

polenta casserole with italian sausage & basil
Prepare the basic recipe, adding 6–8 torn fresh basil leaves when combining
the polenta and sausage.

variations

long-simmered beef daube

see base recipe page 114

long-simmered beef daube with parsnips
Prepare the basic recipe, adding 2 parsnips, peeled and chopped, with the carrots.

long-simmered beef daube with russet potatoes
Prepare the basic recipe, adding 1 pound russet potatoes, peeled and quartered, for last hour of cooking. Omit egg noodles if preferred.

long-simmered beef daube with shallots
Prepare the basic recipe, replacing the onions with 6–8 peeled shallots.

long-simmered beef daube with orange zest
Prepare the basic recipe, adding 2 teaspoons fresh orange zest with the red wine.

variations

veal parmigiana

see base recipe page 116

chicken parmigiana
Prepare the basic recipe, replacing the veal with 4 skinless, boneless chicken breasts.

eggplant parmigiana
Prepare the basic recipe, replacing veal with 2 medium-sized eggplants, sliced into 1/4-inch-thick slices.

veal parmigiana with mozzarella
Prepare the basic recipe, reducing quantity of evaporated milk to 1/3 cup. Omit evaporated milk and Parmesan topping. Top veal with 8 slices mozzarella cheese. Sprinkle Parmesan on top.

veal parmigiana with herb breadcrumbs
Prepare the basic recipe, adding one more step after dredging in flour. Combine 2 large eggs and 1 teaspoon water and whisk in a shallow dish. Combine 1 1/2 cups dry breadcrumbs, 1/2 cup grated Parmesan, and 1 tablespoon each freshly chopped basil and Italian parsley in another shallow dish. Working with one at a time, dip the flour-coated veal into the egg mixture, and then into the breadcrumb mixture. Proceed with recipe.

poultry casseroles

Something magical happens when you put poultry in a casserole. It soaks up the juices and flavors of other ingredients, with unbelievably moist and tasty results. Whether you have leftovers to use or are looking for a new idea, you'll find it here.

chicken cacciatore

see variations page 143

This is one of those classic dishes where the flavor improves if it is left to sit for a day. It's perfect for making on the weekend and pulling out on a busy weekday night. Serve with pasta, rice, or mashed potatoes.

2 tsp. salt
2 tsp. dried basil
1 tsp. dried thyme
1 tsp. dried oregano
1 tsp. garlic powder
1/2 tsp. freshly ground black pepper
pinch of cayenne pepper
2 lb. skinless, boneless chicken breasts, cut into
    1/2-inch strips

2 tbsp. extra-virgin olive oil
1 medium onion, finely chopped
1 garlic clove, minced
1 medium green bell pepper, julienned
1 (14.5-oz.) can whole tomatoes with liquid
2 tbsp. tomato paste
1/2 cup dry red wine
1 cup low-sodium chicken broth

In a small bowl, combine salt, basil, thyme, oregano, garlic powder, pepper, and cayenne. Rub chicken slices with half the spice mixture. Heat oil in large, heavy-based frying pan over medium-high heat. Brown chicken pieces until golden on all sides. Transfer to a plate and set aside. Reduce heat to medium. Sauté onions until soft and translucent, about 4 minutes. Add garlic and green bell pepper. Continue cooking until peppers are tender, about 5 minutes. Add remaining spice mixture and stir to coat. Add tomatoes, tomato paste, red wine, and broth. Stir until tomato paste is well incorporated. Bring to a boil, reduce heat, and return chicken pieces to pan. Simmer until sauce thickens and chicken is cooked through, about 25 minutes.

Serves 4–6

coconut chicken korma

see variations page 144

The longer you marinate the chicken, the more tender this dish will be. Garam masala, a spice mixture used in Indian cooking, is becoming more available in supermarkets, or it can be found in Indian food shops.

2 lb. skinless, boneless chicken breasts, cut into
    bite-sized pieces
1 1/2 cups plain yogurt
4 tbsp. canola oil
1 cup finely chopped onions
1 garlic clove, minced
1 tsp. grated fresh ginger

1 tsp. ground cardamom
1/2 tsp. ground cumin
1 tsp. red chili powder
1 tsp. garam masala powder
1 tbsp. ground coriander
salt and freshly ground black pepper to taste
1/2 cup coconut milk

Place chicken pieces and 1 cup yogurt in a medium-sized bowl. Stir to coat, cover the bowl with plastic wrap, and marinate in refrigerator for at least 1 hour or up to 12 hours. Heat oil in a large frying pan over medium heat. Sauté onions until golden brown, about 6–8 minutes. Add garlic and ginger and cook for 1 minute. Add all the spices and the remaining 1/2 cup yogurt. When liquid from yogurt has almost completely evaporated, add chicken pieces and fry until all sides are brown. Add coconut milk, stir, cover, and reduce heat to low. Simmer for 10–12 minutes, until meat is cooked through and tender.

Serves 4–6

chicken & dumplings

see variations page 145

This comforting chicken stew transforms into a casserole with the addition of quick dumplings cooked on the surface.

1/4 cup all-purpose flour
salt and freshly ground black pepper to taste
2 1/2 lb. skinless, boneless chicken thighs and
    breasts, cut into 1 1/2-inch pieces
2 tbsp. extra-virgin olive oil
1 medium onion, cut into 8 segments
2 carrots, roughly chopped
2 celery stalks, roughly chopped
1 bay leaf

4 cups low-sodium chicken broth
1 1/2 cups all-purpose flour
2 tsp. baking powder
1/2 cup coarse cornmeal
1 tbsp. granulated sugar
1 tsp. kosher salt
1 3/4 cups heavy cream
2 tbsp. finely chopped Italian parsley, to garnish

Place flour in shallow dish and season with salt and pepper. Dredge chicken pieces in flour mixture and set aside. Heat olive oil in a large Dutch oven over medium heat. Brown chicken for 2 minutes per side, then transfer to plate and set aside. Add onion, carrots, celery, and bay leaf. Season with salt and pepper, and cook for 2 minutes. Add chicken broth and bring to a boil. Reduce heat, return chicken to Dutch oven, and simmer for 15 minutes.

To prepare the dumplings, combine flour, baking powder, cornmeal, sugar, and salt in a large bowl. Add cream and stir just until it is incorporated. Remove bay leaf from chicken mixture. Drop dumpling mixture, one heaping tablespoonful at a time, onto hot chicken mixture, being careful not to drop dumplings directly into liquid. Cook, uncovered, for 10 minutes. Cover and simmer for another 10 minutes. Serve in bowls, garnished with parsley.

Serves 4–6

chicken & leeks

see variations page 146

This dish requires only a few minutes' preparation, before it fills your home with an incredible aroma. It's perfect rainy-day food.

1 whole chicken (3–4 lb.)
1/2 lemon
3 leeks, halved and washed thoroughly
1 pint chicken stock (optional)
1/4 cup unsalted butter, melted

2 tbsp. finely chopped Italian parsley
pinch of dried tarragon (or 1 tsp. freshly
    chopped tarragon)
salt and freshly ground black pepper to taste

Preheat oven to 300°F. Remove giblets from chicken cavity, clean chicken, and pat dry. Rub chicken inside and out with the lemon, squeezing juice as you do so. Leave lemon in chicken cavity. Place chicken in large Dutch oven or other heavy-lidded casserole. Place leek halves around chicken. If you prefer a very moist casserole, pour stock over leeks. Use pastry brush to cover chicken with melted butter. Sprinkle all over with parsley, tarragon, salt, and pepper. Insert meat thermometer in thickest part of thigh, taking care to not touch the bone. Place lid on casserole and cook for 2–2 1/2 hours. Cook until meat thermometer reads 180°F, or juice is no longer pink when center of thigh is sliced and drumstick moves easily when lifted.

Let stand for 15 minutes before carving. Serve with leeks and liquid from casserole.

Serves 4–6

chicken potpie

see variations page 147

The perfect way to use up leftover roast chicken, this potpie is pure comfort food.

1 large potato, peeled and cut into small cubes
2 carrots, peeled and cut into small chunks
2 tbsp. unsalted butter
1 chicken stock cube
2 tbsp. all-purpose flour

2 1/4 cups whole milk
1/2 cup frozen peas
2 cups chopped cooked chicken
freshly ground black pepper to taste
pastry for 1 (9-inch) crust

Preheat oven to 375°F. Place potato and carrots in medium saucepan filled with water. Bring water to boil and cook vegetables 5–10 minutes, until tender, but not soft. Remove from heat, drain, and set aside. In medium saucepan, melt butter with chicken stock cube. Use wooden spoon to break up cube. When butter is melted and mixture is smooth, add flour, stirring to form a smooth paste. Cook over low heat for 1 minute. Remove from heat and add milk, stirring constantly. When mixture is smooth, return to burner and cook over medium-low heat for 10 minutes, until sauce thickens. Remove from heat. Stir cooked vegetables, frozen peas, and chicken into sauce. Season with pepper. Butter a 9-inch pie plate and pour in chicken mixture. Moisten edge of pie plate with milk or water. Lay the pastry over chicken mixture, pressing edge down on pie plate to seal, then crimp decoratively. Make 4–6 gashes to allow steam to escape. Bake for 30 minutes or until filling is hot and crust is golden brown. Any leftovers can be refrigerated for up to 3 days.

To make individual potpies, lightly grease 6 (3-inch) ramekins and fill with 1/3–1/2 cup chicken filling. Roll out pastry to 1/4-inch thickness and cut 3-inch rounds. Top ramekins with pastry rounds, glaze the pastry with lightly beaten egg, and make 1 or 2 steam vents.

Serves 4

turkey gougère

see variations page 148

Gougère is the name given to a puff pastry (choux) that is served in a ring around a savory filling. This recipe is by far the most elegant way to make use of turkey leftovers.

3 tbsp. unsalted butter or turkey drippings
4 tbsp. all-purpose flour, plus 1/2 cup
2 cups whole milk
2 tbsp. capers
1/4 tsp. dried sage
pinch of ground nutmeg

2 cups diced cooked turkey
salt and freshly ground black pepper to taste
1/4 cup unsalted butter, melted
1/2 cup water
pinch of salt
1 large egg

Preheat oven to 375°F. To prepare the filling, melt butter or drippings in medium saucepan. Stir in flour until it is a smooth paste, then remove from heat, whisk in milk, and return to medium heat. Bring to a boil and cook, stirring constantly, until mixture thickens, about 5 minutes. Remove from heat. Stir in capers, sage, nutmeg, and diced turkey. Season to taste. To prepare the gougère, stir melted butter and water together in a saucepan over medium-high heat. Bring to a boil. Whisk in 1/2 cup flour with a pinch of salt. When mixture is smooth, switch to a wooden spoon, and stir continuously until it begins to pull away from the sides of the pan. Add the egg and stir until fully incorporated. Pour mixture into a medium casserole, no deeper than 2 inches, or divide evenly between 2–3 smaller dishes. Use a spatula or flat-blade knife to spread the gougère around the base of the casserole. Pour turkey mixture into the middle of the dish and using a fork, pull the edges of the gougère slightly over the filling. Bake for 30–40 minutes, until gougère is puffy and golden brown. Serve immediately.

Serves 2–3

canard creole

see variations page 149

This spicy duck casserole originated in Madagascar. It is wonderful served with rice.

2 (4-lb.) ducks, cut into several pieces
1 tbsp. extra-virgin olive oil
salt
1/2 cup finely chopped onion
2 garlic cloves, minced
2 tbsp. water
4 peppercorns
4 cloves

1 tsp. powdered turmeric
pinch of ground nutmeg
pinch of ground cinnamon
1 tbsp. minced fresh ginger
1 tbsp. all-purpose flour
1 (14.5-oz.) can plum tomatoes, roughly
    chopped, liquid reserved
1/4 cup dry red wine

Remove excess fat, including the fat between skin and meat, from the ducks. Prick the skin with the end of a paring knife. In a large, heavy-based frying pan, heat oil over medium heat. Brown duck pieces in batches, about 2 minutes per side. Transfer to a large Dutch oven. Reserve 2 tablespoons of duck fat in the frying pan, discarding the rest or reserving for another use. Add onion, garlic, water, peppercorns, cloves, turmeric, nutmeg, cinnamon, and ginger to the frying pan. Stir to combine, cover, and cook over medium-low heat for 10 minutes. Remove lid, sprinkle flour over the mixture, and stir. Add tomatoes with their liquid, cover, and simmer for another 15 minutes. Remove lid, add wine, and bring to a boil. Transfer mixture to Dutch oven with the duck pieces, cover, and simmer for 2 hours, or until duck is tender. Using a wooden spoon, skim the fat from the surface before serving.

Serves 6

quail & fennel casserole

see variations page 150

The subtle flavors of quail and fennel complement one another beautifully in this simple but satisfying casserole.

4 whole quail (a total of 1 1/2 lb.)
1 1/2 tsp. salt
3/4 tsp. freshly ground black pepper
2 tbsp. extra-virgin olive oil
2 fennel bulbs, stalks removed and
    roughly chopped

1/2 cup finely chopped red onion
1 garlic clove, minced
1 lemongrass stalk, finely chopped
1 cinnamon stick
1 cup dry white wine

Preheat oven to 350°F. Rinse quail and pat dry. Combine 1/2 teaspoon salt and 1/4 teaspoon pepper in a small bowl and rub over quail. In a large cast-iron frying pan, heat oil over medium-high heat. Sear quail, breast-side down, for 3–4 minutes. Transfer to plate and set aside. Add fennel, red onion, garlic, and remaining salt and pepper to frying pan. Sauté until fennel is tender, about 7 minutes. Add lemongrass, cinnamon, and wine. Bring mixture to a boil, cover, transfer to a casserole dish, and cook in the oven for 20 minutes.

Add quail, breast-side up, to the vegetables, cover, and return to oven for another 20 minutes. Remove from oven, lift lid, allowing water condensation to return to pan, and baste quail with juices from pot. Let sit, uncovered, for 20 minutes before serving.

Serves 2 as a main course or 4 as an appetizer

braised quail with bok choy

see variations page 151

Fresh baby bok choy offsets the rich port wine and curry sauce in this succulent dish.

8 whole quail (3 lb. total)
salt and freshly ground black pepper
8 tbsp. grated lemon zest
4 tbsp. extra-virgin olive oil
1 cup sliced onion
1 carrot, roughly chopped
pinch of ground nutmeg
1/2 tsp. powdered turmeric

1/2 tsp. ground cumin
1/2 tsp. ground coriander
1 bay leaf
1/2 tsp. crumbled dried rosemary
1/2 cup low-sodium chicken broth
1/2 cup port wine
4 baby bok choy, base trimmed, cleaned, and
    cut in half

Rinse quail and pat dry. Season all over with salt and pepper. Fill each cavity with 1 teaspoon lemon zest. Heat oil in large Dutch oven and brown quail for 20 minutes, turning to brown all sides evenly. Transfer quail to plate and set aside. Add onion, remaining lemon zest, and chopped carrot to Dutch oven. Sauté for 5 minutes, until onion is soft and translucent. Return quail to Dutch oven, breast-side up. Combine nutmeg, turmeric, cumin, and coriander in a small bowl. Sprinkle spice mixture over quail and vegetables. Add bay leaf, rosemary, chicken broth, and port wine. Cover Dutch oven and simmer for 40 minutes. Lift lid every 10 minutes, allowing the water from the lid to return to the pot and to baste quail with juices. Skim excess fat from juices with a wooden spoon, if necessary.

In a large pot of boiling water, cook bok choy until tender, about 5–7 minutes. Drain and serve with quail. Ladle sauce from Dutch oven over quail and bok choy before serving.

Serves 4

variations

chicken cacciatore

see base recipe page 127

chicken cacciatore with mushrooms
Prepare the basic recipe, adding 1 cup sliced cremini mushrooms with the garlic and green bell pepper.

spicy chicken cacciatore
Prepare the basic recipe, adding 1/2 teaspoon cayenne pepper and 1/2 teaspoon crushed red pepper flakes after returning chicken to the casserole.

whole-chicken cacciatore
Prepare the basic recipe, replacing chicken breast strips with a 3- to 3 1/2-pound chicken, cut into 8 pieces. Skim fat from sauce just before serving.

chicken cacciatore with capers
Prepare the basic recipe, adding 2 tablespoons capers after returning chicken to the casserole.

chicken cacciatore with soft polenta
Prepare the basic recipe, serving each portion over a serving of soft polenta.
To prepare soft polenta, bring 4 cups water and 1/4 teaspoon salt to a boil. Whisk in 1 cup medium-grain polenta. Lower heat to simmer, add 4 tablespoons unsalted butter, and cook, stirring frequently, for 30 minutes. Stir in 1/4 cup freshly grated Parmesan and serve immediately.

variations

coconut chicken korma

see base recipe page 128

coconut chicken korma with almonds
Prepare the basic recipe, adding 2 tablespoons ground blanched almonds after the coconut milk has been incorporated.

coconut chicken korma with cilantro
Prepare the basic recipe, adding 1/4 cup finely chopped cilantro just before serving.

coconut beef korma
Prepare the basic recipe, replacing the chicken with an equal quantity of stewing beef.

coconut lamb korma
Prepare the basic recipe, replacing the chicken with an equal quantity of boneless lamb shoulder, cut into 1 1/2-inch cubes.

coconut chicken korma with tomatoes
Prepare the basic recipe, adding 3 peeled, seeded, and chopped plum tomatoes after the spices and yogurt have been incorporated.

chicken & dumplings

see base recipe page 131

chicken & dumplings with mushrooms
Prepare the basic recipe, adding 1 cup sliced cremini mushrooms with the carrots and celery.

chicken & dumplings with peas
Prepare the basic recipe, adding 1 cup frozen or fresh peas once the cream has been incorporated.

turkey & dumplings
Prepare the basic recipe, replacing the chicken with turkey breast.

quick chicken & dumplings
Prepare the basic recipe, omitting the dumpling preparation. Replace the flour, baking powder, cornmeal, sugar, salt, and cream with 2 1/2 cups biscuit mix and 2/3 cup milk. Combine until a soft dough forms, then proceed with recipe.

chicken & dumplings with bacon
Prepare the basic recipe, beginning by frying 4–5 slices roughly chopped thick-cut bacon in the Dutch oven. Remove the bacon pieces and set aside. Drain off all but 2 tablespoons bacon fat. Omit olive oil and proceed with recipe. Return bacon to Dutch oven when you add the chicken.

variations

chicken & leeks

see base recipe page 132

chicken & leeks with sausages
Prepare the basic recipe, adding 4–6 pork sausages with the leeks.

chicken & fennel
Prepare the basic recipe, replacing the leeks with 3 fennel bulbs, cleaned, ends trimmed, and cut in half lengthwise.

chicken & leeks with potatoes
Prepare the basic recipe, adding 2 pounds new potatoes, scrubbed, for the last 40 minutes of cooking.

chicken & leeks with thyme
Prepare the basic recipe, replacing the tarragon with 2 fresh sprigs of thyme.

chicken & leeks with carrots
Prepare the basic recipe, adding 4 or 5 roughly chopped carrots for the last 30 minutes of cooking.

variations

chicken potpie

see base recipe page 135

turkey potpie
Prepare the basic recipe, replacing the cooked chicken with cooked turkey.

salmon potpie
Prepare the basic recipe, replacing the chicken stock cube with a fish or vegetable stock cube. Replace the cooked chicken with 2 cups cooked, flaked salmon.

easy chicken potpie
Instead of the basic recipe, combine 1 can condensed cream of chicken soup with 1 cup whole milk over medium heat. Stir in 2 cups cooked chicken and 2 cups mixed frozen vegetables. Season to taste. Pour into buttered 9-inch pie plate and top with 1 sheet pastry. Crimp edges. Make 4–6 gashes to allow steam to escape and bake at 375°F for 30 minutes, or until filling is hot and pastry is golden.

chicken & bacon potpie
Prepare the basic recipe, adding 6 slices fried and crumbled bacon and 1 teaspoon dried oregano to the filling with the cooked chicken.

chicken & leeks potpie
Prepare the basic recipe, adding 3 medium leeks, white and pale green parts sliced, to the potatoes and carrots once the water has boiled. Add 1 tablespoon chopped fresh thyme to the filling.

variations

turkey gougère

see base recipe page 136

chicken gougère
Prepare the basic recipe, replacing the cooked turkey with an equal quantity of cooked chicken.

turkey gougère with peas
Prepare the basic recipe, adding 1/2 cup canned or frozen peas with the capers.

easy turkey gougère
Prepare the basic recipe, replacing the homemade pastry with a package of prepared puff pastry. Thaw according to package instructions, then roll out and cut a circle the same diameter as the casserole dish you are using. Using a paring knife, mark a circle 1 inch from the edge of the pastry, taking care not to cut all the way through the pastry. Place filling inside this line. Proceed with recipe.

turkey gougère with cranberries
Prepare the basic recipe, adding 1/2 cup fresh or frozen cranberries with the cooked turkey.

canard creole

see base recipe page 139

canard creole with green pepper
Prepare the basic recipe, adding 1/2 cup chopped green bell peppers with the onions and garlic.

canard creole with mace
Prepare the basic recipe, adding 1/4 teaspoon ground mace with the nutmeg and cinnamon.

canard creole with pancetta
Fry 6 ounces cubed pancetta until crisp. Prepare the basic recipe, transferring pancetta to Dutch oven before browning duck.

canard creole with orange
Prepare the basic recipe, adding the juice and zest of 1/2 an orange with the tomatoes.

variations

quail & fennel casserole

see base recipe page 140

quail & fennel casserole with raisins
Prepare the basic recipe, adding 1/4 cup raisins with the wine.

cornish hen & fennel casserole
Prepare the basic recipe, replacing the quail with Rock Cornish hens.

grouse & fennel casserole
Prepare the basic recipe, replacing the quail with grouse.

quail & fennel casserole with olives
Prepare the basic recipe, garnishing each portion of quail with 2 tablespoons chopped Niçoise olives.

variations

braised quail with bok choy

see base recipe page 142

braised quail with shallots & bok choy
Prepare the basic recipe, replacing the onions with 4–6 peeled shallots.

braised quail with currants & bok choy
Prepare the basic recipe, adding 1/4 cup currants to the port wine and
setting aside for 30 minutes before preparing the quail. Add currants and
port to the casserole together.

braised quail with apricots & bok choy
Prepare the basic recipe, adding 8 dried apricots to the port wine and setting
aside for 30 minutes before preparing the quail. Before adding bay leaf
to the casserole, place 1 apricot on each quail breast.

braised quail with leeks
Prepare the basic recipe, omitting bok choy. Trim and julienne 3–4 leeks
and cook in a large pot of boiling water until tender, 4–5 minutes. Serve
with the quail.

fish & seafood casseroles

Fish and seafood make delicious casseroles, from rustic seaside stews to retro favorites, and creamy comfort food to fresh and aromatic dishes. For the best results, use the freshest seafood available.

new tuna casserole

see variations page 169

The classic tuna casserole called for condensed cream of mushroom soup. Our new tuna casserole has a creamy made-from-scratch sauce instead.

1/4 cup unsalted butter
1/4 cup all-purpose flour
1 1/2 cups whole milk
1 1/2 cups grated sharp cheddar
salt and freshly ground black pepper to taste

2 cans light chunk tuna, drained and flaked
3 cups uncooked macaroni
1 cup frozen peas
1/2 cup dry breadcrumbs

Preheat oven to 375°F. To prepare the sauce, melt butter in small saucepan over low heat. Stir in flour until it is a smooth paste, then remove from heat, whisk in milk, and return to medium heat. Bring to a boil and cook, stirring constantly, until mixture thickens, about 5 minutes. Remove from heat and stir in 1 1/4 cups of the grated cheddar. Stir until cheese has melted and sauce is smooth. Season with salt and pepper. Add tuna to the sauce, stir, and set aside.

In a large saucepan of boiling salted water, cook macaroni, following package directions, until al dente. Add frozen peas for the last minute of cooking. Drain and add to tuna mixture. Spread mixture into a large, lightly buttered casserole. Smooth top and sprinkle with breadcrumbs and remaining cheese. Bake for 25 minutes, until top is golden and bubbly.

Serves 4–6

cod & potato bake

see variations page 170

This delectable Portuguese specialty requires advance planning, because the salt cod needs to be soaked for 24 hours before preparing the casserole.

1 lb. skinless dried salt cod
4 russet potatoes, peeled and halved
2 tbsp. extra-virgin olive oil
1 large Spanish onion, thinly sliced
2 tbsp. unsalted butter
2 tbsp. all-purpose flour

1 1/2 cups whole milk
salt and freshly ground black pepper to taste
pinch of cayenne pepper
1/3 cup finely chopped Italian parsley
1 cup grated Gruyère cheese

Rinse salt cod well and place in large bowl. Cover with cold water. Cover bowl with plastic wrap and refrigerate for 24 hours, changing the water every 3–4 hours.

Drain cod, rinse once more, and pat dry. Transfer fish to a deep frying pan and cover with water. Bring to a boil over medium-high heat. Reduce to a simmer and cook for another 4–5 minutes. Drain and pat dry. Flake cod, taking care to remove any bones, and place in large bowl.

Preheat oven to 350°F. In a large saucepan of salted water, bring potatoes to a boil. Cook until just tender, about 15 minutes. Drain and slice thinly. Gently combine with cod. Heat olive oil in large, heavy-based frying pan. Add onions and sauté until soft and golden, about 7 minutes. Add to potato and cod mixture.

To prepare the sauce, melt butter in small saucepan over low heat. Stir in flour until it is a smooth paste, then remove from heat, whisk in milk, and return to medium heat. Bring to a boil and cook, stirring constantly, until mixture thickens, about 5 minutes. Remove from heat. Season with salt, pepper, and cayenne. Gently stir into cod mixture. Transfer mixture to a medium-size casserole. Sprinkle with parsley and cover with grated cheese. Bake for 35–40 minutes, until bubbly and golden.

Serves 4–6

scalloped salmon

see variations page 171

This family-friendly dish is a great way to get your dose of omega-3.

1 1/2 cups flaked poached salmon
1 1/2 cups coarse cracker crumbs
   (34 soda crackers)
1/2 cup finely chopped celery
2 cloves garlic, minced
1 large onion, finely chopped
1 yellow bell pepper, seeded and chopped

1/2 cup finely chopped Italian parsley
1/4 tsp. dried thyme
salt and freshly ground black pepper to taste
1/3 cup unsalted butter, melted
2 eggs, lightly beaten
2 tbsp. unsalted butter

Preheat oven to 375°F.

In medium bowl, combine salmon, cracker crumbs, chopped vegetables, parsley, and thyme. Season with salt and pepper. Add melted butter and eggs, and combine well. Spread mixture in a medium-sized, lightly buttered casserole. Dot with remaining 2 tablespoons butter. Bake for 30 minutes, until hot and slightly puffed.

Serves 4

baked snapper with mushrooms

see variations page 172

An easy, layered fish casserole that will please everyone at the table.

1 1/2 lb. red snapper fillets, cut into 6 pieces
2 tbsp. fresh lemon juice
pinch of Spanish paprika
salt and freshly ground black pepper to taste
1 1/2 cups sliced cremini mushrooms
5 tbsp. unsalted butter

3 tbsp. all-purpose flour
1 1/4 cups whole milk
1/4 cup dry white wine
1/2 tsp. salt
1 cup grated Emmental cheese

Preheat oven to 400°F. Place fish portions in a single layer in a lightly buttered shallow casserole. Drizzle lemon juice over fish and sprinkle with paprika, salt, and pepper. Bake for 10 minutes.

While fish is baking, sauté mushrooms in 2 tablespoons butter in a small frying pan until softened, about 4 minutes. Set aside.

In a medium saucepan, melt remaining 3 tablespoons butter over medium heat. Add flour and stir until it is a smooth paste. Remove from heat and whisk in milk and 1/2 teaspoon salt. Return to burner, add wine, then bring mixture to a boil. Cook until mixture thickens, about 5 minutes.

Drain any liquid from fish. Arrange mushrooms over fish. Pour sauce over mushrooms and sprinkle grated Emmental on top. Return to oven for 20 minutes, until bubbly.

Serves 6

sole with stuffing

see variations page 173

The stuffing in this dish is actually used as a topping—one that makes the fish incredibly moist and flavorful.

2 tbsp. unsalted butter
1 cup finely chopped onion
3 slices day-old bread, torn into small pieces
1/4 tsp. dried thyme

2 tsp. finely chopped Italian parsley
1 tsp. grated lemon zest
1 egg
4 sole fillets

Preheat oven to 350°F. To prepare the stuffing, melt butter in heavy-based, medium-sized frying pan. Add onion and sauté until soft and translucent, about 5 minutes. Combine sautéed onion with torn bread, thyme, parsley, lemon zest, and egg in mixing bowl. Lightly butter medium-sized casserole. Arrange fillets in a single layer. Spread stuffing over fillets and bake for 20–30 minutes, until fish is opaque and flakes easily.

Serves 4

crab casserole

see variations page 174

This rich casserole makes a wonderful alternative to individual crab cakes. It can be served with a peppery mix of greens for a light lunch, or with a sliced baguette for a delicious appetizer.

1 tbsp. unsalted butter
2 tbsp. finely chopped onion
1 carrot, finely chopped
1 celery stick, finely chopped
1/2 cup chicken broth
1/4 cup dry white wine
large pinch of dried tarragon

1/2 cup heavy cream
1 1/2 cups fresh lump crabmeat, picked over
1 tsp. fresh lemon juice
pinch of cayenne pepper
salt and freshly ground black pepper to taste
1/4 cup freshly grated Parmesan

Preheat broiler. In heavy-based, medium-sized saucepan, melt butter over low heat. Add onion, carrot, and celery, and increase heat to medium. Stir for 1 minute. Stir in broth, wine, and tarragon. Bring mixture to a boil, and cook until liquid is reduced to 1 tablespoon. Add cream and return to a boil. Stir until sauce thickens, about 2 minutes. Remove from heat and stir in crabmeat, lemon juice, and cayenne. Season to taste with salt and pepper. Transfer mixture to a small, lightly buttered casserole. Sprinkle with Parmesan and broil for 2 minutes, until cheese is melted and casserole is bubbly and golden.

Serves 3–4 as light lunch or appetizer

shrimp & cauliflower gratin

see variations page 175

Cheesy cauliflower, with the addition of succulent shrimp, makes a great meal-in-one.

1 large cauliflower
1/4 cup unsalted butter
1/2 onion, finely chopped
1/4 cup all-purpose flour

1 1/2 cups whole milk
1 cup grated sharp cheddar
salt and freshly ground black pepper, to taste
1 cup peeled and deveined, cooked shrimp

Trim cauliflower, discard stalk, wash, and cook whole (or cut into florets if you prefer) in salted boiling water until tender, about 7 minutes. Drain and place in a lightly buttered 9-inch glass pie plate, or other small casserole.

Preheat oven to 375°F. To prepare the sauce, melt butter in small saucepan over medium-low heat. Add onion and cook until it is soft and translucent, about 5 minutes. Stir in flour to form a paste, then remove from heat, whisk in milk, and return to medium heat. Bring to a boil and cook, stirring constantly, until mixture thickens, about 5 minutes. Remove from heat and stir in 1/2 cup grated cheddar. Stir until cheese has melted. Season with salt and pepper. Fold shrimp into sauce, and pour sauce over cauliflower. Sprinkle with remaining cheese. Bake for 20 minutes, until golden and bubbly.

Serves 4

bouillabaisse

see variations page 176

A classic French stew that is a feast for seafood lovers.

3/4 cup extra-virgin olive oil
2 medium onions, thinly sliced
2 leeks, cleaned, white and pale green
    parts julienned
3 ripe, fresh tomatoes, peeled, seeded
    and chopped
4 cloves garlic, minced
1 sprig fennel leaf
1 sprig fresh thyme
1 bay leaf

1 tsp. grated lemon zest
9 cups water
3 lb. fresh cod fillets, cut into 2-inch pieces
1 lb. small clams, such as littlenecks
1 lb. large scallops
3/4 lb. mussels, cleaned and debearded
3/4 lb. fresh shrimp, peeled and deveined
salt and freshly ground black pepper to taste
1/4 cup finely chopped Italian parsley,
    to garnish

In a large saucepan, heat olive oil over medium heat. Add onions, leeks, chopped tomatoes, and garlic. Cook, stirring occasionally, for 5 minutes, until vegetables are tender. Add fennel, thyme, bay leaf, and lemon zest. Add 9 cups water and bring to a boil. Let simmer, uncovered, for 20 minutes, until liquid has reduced a bit. Add cod and cook for 2 minutes. Add clams, scallops, mussels, and shrimp. Simmer until all shells have opened, scallops are opaque, and shrimp is pink, about 6 minutes. Cod should be opaque and tender, but still firm. Taste and adjust seasonings as necessary. Serve in bowls, sprinkled with chopped parsley.

Serves 12

seafood gumbo

see variations page 177

This recipe calls for filé powder, a seasoning made from the dried leaves of the sassafras tree. Serve gumbo on a bed of rice.

1/4 cup, plus 2 tbsp. unsalted butter
2 cups finely chopped onions
3/4 cup finely chopped celery
3 cloves garlic, minced
1/4 cup all-purpose flour
16 oz. canned whole tomatoes, roughly chopped, liquid reserved
1 tsp. granulated sugar
2 tbsp. finely chopped Italian parsley
1 sprig fresh thyme

2 bay leaves
1/2 tsp. cayenne pepper
salt and freshly ground black pepper, to taste
1 lb. andouille sausage, cut into 1/2-inch pieces
1/2 lb. fresh lump crabmeat, picked over
1 lb. medium shrimp, peeled and deveined
1/2 tsp. hot pepper sauce
1/4 cup Worcestershire sauce
juice of 1/2 lemon
filé powder for serving

In a large, heavy-based frying pan over medium heat, melt 2 tablespoons butter. Add onions, and cook for 2 minutes. Add celery and garlic and continue cooking until onions are golden brown, about 6 minutes. Set aside. In a large Dutch oven, melt remaining 1/4 cup butter over medium heat. Add flour and cook, stirring constantly, until paste turns a brownish-red color (roux). Transfer onion mixture to Dutch oven, stir, and add 8 cups water, the tomatoes, and sugar. Stir in parsley, thyme, bay leaves, cayenne, salt, and pepper. Bring to a boil, reduce heat to simmer, and cook for 2 1/2 hours, uncovered. Stir gumbo occasionally as it simmers. Add sausage, crabmeat, and shrimp, and simmer for another 10 minutes, until sausage is cooked through and shrimp is pink. Stir in hot sauce, Worcestershire sauce, and lemon juice. Remove bay leaf and serve in bowls, sprinkling each serving with a pinch of filé powder.

Serves 10

variations

new tuna casserole

see base recipe page 153

new tuna casserole with corn
Prepare the basic recipe, adding 1/2 cup fresh or frozen corn with the peas.

new tuna casserole with fried onions
Prepare the basic recipe, topping the casserole with 1/2 cup prepared fried onions before baking.

new tuna casserole with egg noodles
Prepare the basic recipe, replacing the macaroni with an equal quantity of broad egg noodles. Cook according to package directions.

new tuna casserole with dijon mustard
Prepare the basic recipe, adding 1 tablespoon Dijon mustard with the flour when making the sauce.

classic tuna casserole
Prepare the basic recipe, omitting sauce preparation. Replace the butter, flour, milk, and 1 1/4 cups cheddar with 1 can condensed cream of mushroom soup.

variations

cod & potato bake

see base recipe page 154

salmon & potato bake
Prepare the basic recipe, replacing the cod with 1 1/2 pounds salmon fillet. Omit soaking overnight, just begin with cooking the salmon in water in frying pan.

tilapia & potato bake
Prepare the basic recipe, replacing the cod with 1 1/2 pounds tilapia fillet. Omit soaking overnight, just begin with cooking the tilapia in water in frying pan.

cod & potato bake with olives
Prepare the basic recipe, adding 1/2 cup pitted black olives with the potatoes.

cod & potato bake with corn
Prepare the basic recipe, adding 1/2 cup corn with the potatoes.

sole & potato bake
Prepare the basic recipe, replacing the cod with 1 1/2 pounds sole fillet. Omit soaking overnight, just begin with cooking the sole in water in frying pan.

variations

scalloped salmon

see base recipe page 157

scalloped crab
Prepare the basic recipe, replacing the salmon with an equal quantity of fresh lump crabmeat, picked over for shell pieces.

scalloped tuna
Prepare the basic recipe, replacing the salmon with 2 cans white albacore tuna packed in water, drained and flaked.

quick scalloped salmon
Prepare the basic recipe, replacing the fresh salmon with 2 cans salmon, flaked.

scalloped salmon with green pepper
Prepare the basic recipe, replacing the yellow bell pepper with an equal quantity of green bell pepper.

scalloped salmon with dill
Prepare the basic recipe, replacing the thyme with 2 teaspoons finely chopped fresh dill.

variations

baked snapper with mushrooms

see base recipe page 158

baked snapper with mushrooms & olives
Prepare the basic recipe, arranging 1/4 cup chopped black pitted olives over the mushrooms before sprinkling the cheese.

baked snapper with artichoke hearts
Prepare the basic recipe, arranging a 14-ounce can artichoke hearts, drained and roughly chopped, over the mushrooms before sprinkling the cheese.

baked snapper with hardboiled eggs
Prepare the basic recipe, folding 2 hardboiled eggs, chopped, into the sauce once it has thickened.

baked snapper with shrimp
Prepare the basic recipe, adding 1 pound shrimp, peeled and deveined, around the fish pieces after they have baked for 10 minutes.

variations

sole with stuffing

see base recipe page 161

cod with stuffing
Prepare the basic recipe, replacing the sole with cod fillets.

sole with mushroom stuffing
Prepare the basic recipe, adding 1 cup chopped cremini mushrooms
with the onion when preparing the stuffing.

tilapia with stuffing
Prepare the basic recipe, replacing the sole with tilapia fillets.

trout with stuffing
Prepare the basic recipe, replacing the sole with trout fillets.

variations

crab casserole

see base recipe page 162

crab casserole with corn
Prepare the basic recipe, adding 1 cup fresh or frozen corn to the mixture with the crabmeat.

crab casserole with pecorino
Prepare the basic recipe, replacing the Parmesan with an equal quantity of grated Pecorino.

crab casserole with dill
Prepare the basic recipe, replacing the pinch of dried tarragon with a large pinch of finely chopped fresh dill.

crab casserole with spinach
Prepare the basic recipe, adding 2 cups roughly chopped fresh spinach leaves once the wine mixture has reduced.

crab casserole with herbed breadcrumbs
Prepare the basic recipe, combining 1/2 cup dry breadcrumbs, 1/2 teaspoon dried basil, and 1/4 teaspoon dried thyme with the Parmesan before sprinkling over casserole.

variations

shrimp & cauliflower gratin

see base recipe page 165

shrimp & cauliflower gratin with dill
Prepare the basic recipe, folding 1 tablespoon finely chopped fresh dill into the sauce with the shrimp.

shrimp & cauliflower gratin with breadcrumbs
Prepare the basic recipe, sprinkling the casserole with 1/2 cup dry breadcrumbs before baking.

shrimp & cauliflower gratin with tomato
Prepare the basic recipe, arranging 5 or 6 tomato slices over the casserole before baking.

crab & cauliflower gratin
Prepare the basic recipe, replacing the shrimp with an equal amount of fresh or canned crabmeat, picked over for shells.

variations

bouillabaisse

see base recipe page 166

bouillabaisse with saffron
Prepare the basic recipe, adding a pinch of saffron with the water.

bouillabaisse with kale
Prepare the basic recipe, adding 4 cups kale, stems trimmed and roughly chopped, just before adding the fish. Stir to combine.

bouillabaisse with orange zest
Prepare the basic recipe, replacing the lemon zest with zest of 1/2 an orange.

bouillabaisse with sea bass
Prepare the basic recipe, replacing the cod with sea bass.

bouillabaisse with rouille
Prepare the basic recipe, then serve each portion with 1/2 teaspoon of rouille. To prepare the rouille, combine in a food processor 1 tablespoon hot fish stock or clam juice with 2 peeled cloves garlic, 1 small red chile pepper, 1/2 teaspoon salt, and 1 slice white bread, torn into small pieces. Blend until smooth. With processor still running, drizzle in olive oil and stop as soon as oil is incorporated (about 1–3 tablespoons).

seafood gumbo

see base recipe page 168

seafood gumbo with okra
Prepare the basic recipe, adding 1 pound chopped okra, which has been fried in 2 tablespoons vegetable oil for 30–40 minutes over very low heat. Add okra to gumbo with water and tomato.

seafood gumbo with chicken
Prepare the basic recipe, replacing the sausage with 2 cups leftover cooked chicken. Add the chicken with the crabmeat and shrimp.

seafood gumbo with hardboiled eggs
Prepare the basic recipe, stirring 4 hardboiled eggs, chopped, into the gumbo just before serving.

seafood gumbo with catfish
Prepare the basic recipe, adding 1 1/2 pounds catfish fillets, cut into 1 1/2-inch chunks. Add the catfish with the sausage and crabmeat.

vegetarian & vegan casseroles

The vegetarian casseroles in this chapter are meatless; however, they may contain eggs and dairy products. To keep these dishes strictly vegetarian, be sure to use certified vegetarian cheeses (those that do not contain rennet). The vegan casseroles contain no animal products whatsoever.

autumn squash casserole

see variations page 195

This gorgeous dish brings fall colors to the table — perfect for a Thanksgiving feast or autumn potluck.

2 medium-large butternut squash
1/2 tsp. extra-virgin olive oil
3 tbsp. unsalted butter
1 cup finely chopped onion
2 cloves garlic, minced
1 cup seeded and chopped red bell pepper

2 eggs, lightly beaten
1 cup buttermilk
1/2 cup crumbled feta cheese
1 tsp. salt
freshly ground black pepper to taste

Preheat oven to 375°F. Trim ends off squash, cut in half lengthwise, and remove seeds. Wipe a baking sheet with the olive oil and arrange squash flesh-side down. Bake until squash is soft, about 40–45 minutes, depending on thickness of squash. Set aside to cool.

In a medium-sized, heavy-based frying pan, melt butter over medium heat. Add onions and cook for 5 minutes, until they are soft and translucent. Add garlic and cook for another minute. Stir in bell peppers and sauté for another 4–5 minutes, until onions are golden brown and peppers are crisp-tender. Set aside.

In a large mixing bowl, whisk eggs and buttermilk. Add feta. Scrape cooled flesh out of squash skins and mash with a fork. Add to buttermilk mixture and stir to combine. Fold in onion mixture. Add salt and pepper. Spread mixture in medium-sized, lightly buttered casserole. Bake for 25–30 minutes, until casserole is heated through and feta is beginning to melt.

Serves 4

leek & barley casserole

see variations page 196

This hearty casserole can be served on its own as a meal, or as an accompaniment to roast meats or fish.

1 large leek, white and pale green parts
1 medium onion
2 large carrots
2 tomatoes

1 cup raw barley
3 cups vegetable stock
4 oz. aged cheddar, cubed
4 oz. feta, crumbled

Preheat oven to 350°F. Rinse leek thoroughly, then cut into matchstick-size pieces. Clean and chop onion, carrots, and tomatoes. Place vegetables in large casserole with tight-fitting lid. Rinse barley and add to casserole dish with vegetable stock. Stir so that vegetables and barley are covered in stock. Cover casserole and bake for 45–50 minutes. Remove from oven and stir in cheeses. Return to oven, uncovered, for 20 minutes, or until almost all the stock has been absorbed.

Serves 4–6

eggplant & zucchini bake

see variations page 197

A delightful autumn dish, best served with a rustic, crusty loaf for soaking up any juices.

1 large eggplant, in 1/2-inch-thick slices	2 tbsp. finely chopped Italian parsley
salt	fresly ground black pepper to taste
2 tbsp. extra-virgin olive oil	2 small zucchini, sliced lengthwise
1 large onion, finely chopped	1/4 cup all-purpose flour
2 garlic cloves, minced	5–6 tbsp. sunflower oil or canola oil
1 (28-oz.) can whole tomatoes with liquid	12 oz. mozzarella, grated
3–4 basil leaves, roughly torn	1/4 cup freshly grated Parmesan

Arrange eggplant slices in a single layer on paper towels. Sprinkle with salt and set aside for 30 minutes. Flip slices, salt, and set aside for another 30 minutes. In a large, heavy-based frying pan, heat olive oil over medium heat. Add onion and garlic and sauté for 4 minutes. Stir in tomatoes, breaking them up into smaller pieces. Add half the basil and half the parsley, and season with salt and pepper. Bring to a boil, reduce heat, and simmer for 25 minutes, until sauce has thickened. Remove from heat and set aside. Preheat oven to 350°F. Rinse eggplant slices with cold water and pat dry. Dredge eggplant and zucchini slices in flour, shaking off excess. In a separate frying pan, heat 2 tablespoons sunflower or canola oil until it begins to shimmer. Fry eggplant and zucchini in batches until golden brown, adding more oil as needed. Lay slices on paper toweling. Lightly butter a 9x9-inch casserole. Cover bottom of casserole with a single layer of eggplant and zucchini. Cover with half the sauce and half the grated mozzarella. Sprinkle with remaining basil and parsley. Add another layer of eggplant and zucchini slices, cover with remaining sauce, then cover with remaining mozzarella. Sprinkle top with Parmesan. Bake for 30 minutes, until golden on top and bubbly.

Serves 4–6

chilaquile casserole

see variations page 198

One portion of this amazing, Mexican-inspired layered dish provides a healthy serving of all five food groups.

1 tbsp. extra-virgin olive oil
1 cup finely chopped onions
1 cup chopped tomato
1 1/2 cups corn kernels, fresh or frozen
1 (15-oz.) can black beans, drained and rinsed
2 tbsp. fresh lime juice
1 tsp. salt
1/2 tsp. freshly ground black pepper

2 cups rinsed, trimmed, and chopped fresh spinach
2 cups crushed tortilla chips
8 oz. sharp cheddar cheese
2 cups prepared salsa
1/4 cup finely chopped fresh cilantro, to serve
1/2 cup sour cream, to serve

Preheat oven to 350°F. Heat oil in a large saucepan over medium heat. Add onions and sauté for 5 minutes, until soft and translucent. Stir in tomatoes, corn, black beans, lime juice, salt, and pepper. Continue to cook for another 10 minutes. In a large saucepan of boiling water, blanch spinach for 1–2 minutes. Drain and set aside.

Lightly butter an 8x8-inch casserole. To layer the chilaquile, spread half the crushed tortilla chips on the bottom, then cover with the black bean mixture. Sprinkle with 2/3 cup grated cheddar, then layer the blanched spinach on top. Spread half the salsa over the spinach. Top with the remaining tortilla chips, then the remaining salsa, and finish with the remaining cheddar. Bake for 40 minutes, until bubbly. Serve with cilantro and sour cream.

Serves 6

cheese strata

see variations page 199

Try this tasty casserole for a weekend breakfast or a special brunch.

8 slices French bread, cut into 1/2-inch strips,
   crusts removed
1 1/2 cups grated sharp cheddar
1 1/2 cups grated Gruyère
2 tbsp. freshly chopped dill
4 eggs

2 cups whole milk
2 tbsp. unsalted butter, melted
pinch of cayenne pepper
pinch of ground nutmeg
1/2 tsp. salt
1/4 tsp. freshly ground black pepper

Lightly butter an 8x8-inch casserole and arrange half the bread on the bottom. Combine the cheeses in a medium bowl. Spread half the cheese blend over the layer of bread. Sprinkle chopped dill over cheese. Arrange remaining bread over the dill and top with remaining cheese. In same bowl, whisk eggs, milk, melted butter, cayenne, nutmeg, salt, and pepper. Pour egg mixture all over bread and cheese. Cover casserole with plastic wrap and refrigerate for 6–12 hours.

Preheat oven to 325°F. Bake for 1 hour, until puffy and golden. Transfer dish to wire rack and cool for 10 minutes before serving.

Serves 4–6

swiss bean casserole

see variations page 200

A decadent way to serve beans, this rich casserole will have guests asking for more.

4 tbsp. unsalted butter
1 tsp. salt
1 tsp. sugar
2 tbsp. all-purpose flour
1/4 tsp. freshly ground black pepper
pinch of ground nutmeg

1/2 cup finely chopped onions
1 cup sour cream
3 lb. haricot verts (fresh green beans)
1 cup grated Emmental cheese
1/4 cup dried breadcrumbs

Preheat oven to 400°F. In a large saucepan, melt 2 tablespoons butter over low heat. Add salt, sugar, flour, pepper, nutmeg, and onions. Stir in sour cream and cook until mixture is hot. Remove from heat.

Trim beans and cut into 1-inch pieces. Measure 6 cups. In a large pot of salted boiling water, cook beans until crisp-tender, about 7 minutes. Fold beans into sour cream mixture and transfer to a medium-sized, lightly buttered casserole. Melt remaining 2 tablespoons butter and combine with grated cheese and breadcrumbs. Sprinkle over beans and bake for 20 minutes.

Serves 4–6

broccoli & mushroom noodle bake

see variations page 201

Cremini mushrooms and broccoli take center stage in this hearty vegetarian dish.

2 tbsp. unsalted butter
1 large onion, finely chopped
2 cups chopped cremini mushrooms
4 cups broccoli florets and peeled and
    sliced stalks
salt and freshly ground black pepper to taste
1/4 cup dry white wine
3 eggs

3 cups ricotta cheese
1 cup plain yogurt
pinch of cayenne pepper
pinch of ground nutmeg
3 cups uncooked broad egg noodles
1/2 cup dry breadcrumbs
1 cup grated sharp cheddar cheese

Preheat oven to 350°F. In large, heavy-based frying pan, melt 1 1/2 tablespoons butter. Add onions, mushrooms, and broccoli, and sauté for 6–8 minutes, until onions and mushrooms are soft and broccoli is tender. Season with salt and pepper, toss with white wine, and set aside. In a mixing bowl, whisk eggs, ricotta, yogurt, cayenne, and nutmeg together. Set aside. In a large pot of boiling salted water, cook noodles following package instructions for al dente. Drain and toss with remaining 1/2 tablespoon butter.

Fold vegetables into egg-yogurt mixture. Stir in noodles and 1/4 cup breadcrumbs. Spread mixture into large (9x13-inch) lightly buttered casserole. Combine remaining breadcrumbs with cheese and spread over casserole. Cover with aluminum foil and bake for 30 minutes. Remove foil and bake for another 15 minutes, until heated through and bubbly.

Serves 6

chickpea tagine with currant couscous

see variations page 202

A tagine is an earthenware dish from North Africa, ingeniously designed with a self-basting conical lid. It's also the name for the stew cooked in this dish. If you do not have a tagine (dish), a large saucepan with a close-fitting lid will work equally well when making this vegan recipe. Just be sure to let the condensation from the lid return to the pot when lifting the lid.

1/4 cup extra-virgin olive oil
1 medium onion, finely chopped
3 garlic cloves, minced
1/2 tsp. ground cumin
1/2 tsp. powdered turmeric
1/4 tsp. cayenne pepper
1 tsp. Spanish paprika
2 tsp. tomato paste
1 tsp. apricot jam
2 tbsp. finely chopped Italian parsley
2 tbsp. finely chopped cilantro

1 cup water, plus more if necessary
1 pint cherry tomatoes
1 (15-oz.) can chickpeas, drained and rinsed
1 tsp. salt
pinch of freshly ground black pepper
1 cup couscous
1 cup vegetable stock
1/3 cup currants
1/3 cup pine nuts
1/4 cup finely chopped mint

Heat oil in a tagine or large saucepan over medium-low heat. Sauté onions until soft and translucent, about 5 minutes. Add garlic and cook for 1 minute, then add cumin, turmeric, and cayenne. Stir constantly for 1 minute. Add paprika, tomato paste, apricot jam, and 1 tablespoon each parsley and cilantro. Stir to combine. Add water, tomatoes, and chickpeas. Stir, season with salt and pepper, and cover. Simmer for 15–20 minutes, until heated through

and tomatoes have popped and softened. Keep warm until serving time. Five minutes before serving, prepare couscous. Bring vegetable stock to a boil in a small pot with a tight-fitting lid. Remove from heat, add couscous, and stir. Cover and let sit for 5 minutes. Fluff couscous with fork, then add currants, pine nuts, and mint. Fluff again and serve with tagine.

Serves 4

savoy cabbage & kale casserole with tofu

see variations page 203

A wonderful winter casserole, this vegan dish makes good use of cold-weather vegetables, with a delicious crumbled tofu topping.

5 tbsp. extra-virgin olive oil
2 medium onions, thinly sliced
4 cups Savoy cabbage, cored and cut crosswise
    into thin slices
4 cups roughly chopped kale leaves, stems and
    ribs removed
3 carrots, julienned
1 cup water

2 tbsp. tamari sauce
3/4 tsp. salt
2/3 cup dry breadcrumbs
2/3 cup drained and roughly chopped firm tofu
2 tsp. dried basil
1 1/2 tsp. dried oregano
1 tsp. Spanish paprika
2 garlic cloves, minced

Preheat oven to 350°F. In a wok or large frying pan with deep sides, heat 2 tablespoons oil over medium heat. Sauté onions until beginning to brown, about 7 minutes. Add cabbage, kale, carrots, water, tamari, and 1/2 teaspoon salt. Stir, cover, and cook for about 8 minutes, stirring occasionally. When greens are tender, transfer mixture to a large, lightly oiled casserole. Pulse breadcrumbs, tofu, basil, oregano, paprika, garlic, and remaining 1/4 teaspoon salt together in food processor (or mash thoroughly with a fork). Spread tofu mixture over vegetables and bake for 15–20 minutes, until golden brown.

Serves 4–6

variations

autumn squash casserole

see base recipe page 179

autumn squash casserole with sunflower seeds
Prepare the basic recipe, sprinkling the casserole with 1/4 cup toasted and chopped sunflower seeds before baking.

autumn squash casserole with mixed peppers
Prepare the basic recipe, replacing the red bell peppers with an equal quantity of seeded and chopped mixed red and green bell peppers.

autumn squash casserole with pine nuts
Prepare the basic recipe, sprinkling the casserole with 1/4 cup toasted and chopped pine nuts before baking.

autumn squash casserole with tofu
Prepare the basic recipe, adding 1/2 cup crumbled firm tofu with the feta.

acorn squash casserole
Prepare the basic recipe, replacing the butternut squash with an equal quantity of acorn squash.

variations

leek & barley casserole

see base recipe page 180

vegan leek & barley casserole
Prepare the basic recipe, replacing the cheddar and feta with 8 ounces vegan (soy) cheese.

leek & barley casserole with peppers
Prepare the basic recipe, adding 1 large red bell pepper, chopped, with the other vegetables.

leek & barley casserole with chèvre
Prepare the basic recipe, replacing the feta with 4 ounces soft-ripened chèvre.

leek & barley casserole with olives
Prepare the basic recipe, adding 4 ounces sliced black olives with the other vegetables.

leek & barley casserole with broccoli
Prepare the basic recipe, adding 1 head of broccoli, chopped into florets, with the cheeses.

variations

eggplant & zucchini bake

see base recipe page 183

eggplant & zucchini bake with mushrooms
Prepare the basic recipe, adding 1 cup sliced cremini mushrooms with the
onions and garlic.

eggplant & zucchini bake with ricotta
Prepare the basic recipe, replacing the mozzarella with 1 1/2 cups ricotta
cheese. Use the ricotta as directed for the mozzarella.

eggplant & zucchini bake with fontina
Prepare the basic recipe, replacing the mozzarella with 12 ounces sliced
Fontina. Replace the layers of mozzarella with layers of Fontina.

eggplant & zucchini bake with olives
Prepare the basic recipe, adding 1/2 cup pitted and sliced black olives with
the tomatoes.

eggplant & zucchini bake with herbed breadcrumbs
Prepare the basic recipe, replacing the 1/4 cup flour with 1/4 cup dry
herbed breadcrumbs.

variations

chilaquile casserole

see base recipe page 184

chilaquile casserole with kidney beans
Prepare the basic recipe, replacing the black beans with kidney beans.

chilaquile casserole with green onions
Prepare the basic recipe, replacing the chopped cilantro with 1/4 cup chopped green onions.

chilaquile casserole with kale
Prepare the basic recipe, replacing the spinach with an equal quantity of kale, stems trimmed and roughly chopped.

chilaquile casserole with peppers
Prepare the basic recipe, adding 1 cup seeded and chopped red bell pepper with the corn.

chilaquile casserole with cumin & chili
Prepare the basic recipe, adding 1 teaspoon ground cumin and 1/2 teaspoon chili powder with the onions.

variations

cheese strata

see base recipe page 187

cheese strata with basil
Prepare the basic recipe, replacing the dill with fresh basil.

cheese strata with sourdough
Prepare the basic recipe, replacing the French bread with an equal quantity
of sourdough bread.

cheese strata with spinach
Prepare the basic recipe, adding 1 cup roughly chopped fresh spinach to
the egg mixture.

cheese strata with cream cheese
Prepare the basic recipe, adding 1 cup cubed cream cheese to the
egg mixture.

cheese strata with tomatoes
Prepare the basic recipe, adding 8 tomato slices, arranging one over each
slice of bread in the bottom layer, and the others over the top bread slices.

variations

swiss bean casserole

see base recipe page 188

swiss bean casserole with cheddar
Prepare the basic recipe, replacing the Emmental with an equal quantity of grated sharp cheddar cheese.

mixed bean casserole
Prepare the basic recipe, replacing the beans with an equal quantity of mixed fresh beans, using a blend of types and colors.

swiss bean casserole with edamame
Prepare the basic recipe, reducing amount of French beans by 1 cup and adding 1 cup of peeled edamame.

swiss bean casserole with sage
Prepare the basic recipe, adding 1 tablespoon freshly chopped sage to the sour cream mixture.

broccoli & mushroom noodle bake

see base recipe page 191

broccoli & mushroom rice bake
Prepare the basic recipe, replacing the cooked noodles with 3 cups of cooked brown rice.

broccoli & portobello noodle bake
Prepare the basic recipe, replacing the cremini mushrooms with an equal quantity of diced portobello mushrooms.

rapini & mushroom noodle bake
Prepare the basic recipe, replacing the broccoli with 5–6 stalks of rapini (broccoli rabe), roughly chopped.

broccoli & mushroom orzo bake
Prepare the basic recipe, replacing the cooked egg noodles with 2 cups of cooked orzo.

variations

chickpea tagine with currant couscous

see base recipe page 192

chickpea & butternut squash tagine with currant couscous
Prepare the basic recipe, adding 1 pound butternut squash. Peel, seed, and cube the squash and increase simmering time to 30 minutes, or until squash is tender. Add the tomatoes to the squash after it's been simmering for about 10 minutes.

chickpea & zucchini tagine with currant couscous
Prepare the basic recipe, adding 1 small zucchini, ends trimmed and diced, with the tomatoes.

chickpea & kale tagine with currant couscous
Prepare the basic recipe, adding 2 cups roughly chopped and trimmed kale with the tomatoes.

chickpea & eggplant tagine with currant couscous
Prepare the basic recipe, adding 1 medium eggplant, ends trimmed and diced, with the tomatoes.

savoy cabbage & kale casserole with tofu

see base recipe page 194

savoy cabbage & swiss chard casserole with tofu
Prepare the basic recipe, replacing the kale with Swiss chard.

savoy cabbage & kale casserole with tomatoes
Prepare the basic recipe, topping the cooked greens with 1 cup halved cherry tomatoes before adding tofu topping.

red cabbage & kale casserole
Prepare the basic recipe, replacing the Savoy cabbage with red cabbage.

savoy cabbage & kale casserole with pepitas
Prepare the basic recipe, adding 1/2 cup toasted and chopped pepitas (pumpkin seeds) to the topping mixture before spreading it over the greens.

light casseroles

For times when you are looking for something hearty but health-conscious, this chapter is full of new ideas. These recipes use little or no fat without sacrificing flavor. They are well suited to a low-fat diet, but they can be enjoyed by everyone.

zucchini & polenta bake

see variations page 221

Layers of polenta, tender zucchini, and melted cheese make this light casserole seem decadent.

low-fat cooking spray
2 tbsp. extra-virgin olive oil
2 small zucchini, ends trimmed, finely chopped
1/2 tsp. salt
1/2 tsp. freshly ground black pepper

1 1/2 cups prepared tomato sauce
6-8 fresh basil leaves, roughly torn
14 oz. prepared polenta, sliced into 6 thin slices
1 1/2 cups grated part-skim mozzarella

Preheat oven to 450°F. Lightly coat a large casserole with low-fat cooking spray. Heat oil in a large, heavy-based frying pan over medium-high heat. Add zucchini, salt, and pepper, and cook for 6 minutes, until zucchini are tender and start to brown. Add tomato sauce and stir to combine. Cook until heated through, about 3 minutes. Remove from heat and stir in basil.

Arrange polenta slices in a single layer in casserole. Sprinkle with 3/4 cup grated cheese. Spread zucchini mixture over cheese and sprinkle with remaining cheese. Bake until bubbly, about 15 minutes. Transfer to wire rack to stand for 5 minutes before serving.

Serves 6–8

butternut squash lasagna

see variations page 222

Roasted squash and sautéed mushrooms make this low-fat lasagna a winner.

2 medium butternut squash
2 tbsp. olive oil
3 garlic cloves, minced
2 lb. cremini mushrooms, cleaned and sliced
1/4 tsp. salt
12 oz. evaporated skim milk

1/2 cup thinly sliced shallots
1 tbsp. finely chopped fresh sage
salt and freshly ground black pepper to taste
8 oz. whole wheat lasagna noodles (about 9 noodles)
low-fat cooking spray

Preheat oven to 400°F. Peel 1 squash and cut into 1/2-inch cubes. Set aside. Trim ends off other squash, cut in half lengthwise, and remove seeds. Lightly oil a baking sheet and arrange squash halves flesh-side down. Bake until squash is soft, about 40-45 minutes, depending on thickness of squash. Set aside to cool.

Heat oil in a large frying pan over medium-high heat. Add 2 minced garlic cloves and cook until you can smell the garlic, about 10 seconds. Add mushrooms and 1/4 teaspoon salt. Increase temperature to high and cook, stirring frequently, for 6 minutes. Remove from heat, add cubed squash, and set aside.

In a medium saucepan, combine evaporated milk, shallots, remaining minced garlic, and sage. Bring to a boil, cover, and remove from heat. Scrape roasted squash flesh from skin and mash (discard skin). Add to milk mixture and stir until fully incorporated. Season with salt and pepper and set aside.

In a large pot of salted, boiling water, cook lasagna noodles until just underdone (about 7 minutes). Lightly coat a 9-inch casserole with cooking spray. Spread half the milk and squash mixture onto the bottom of the casserole. Top with 3 noodles, cutting as necessary to make them fit the pan. Spread 1 cup mushroom mixture over the noodles. Cover with a thin layer (1/2 cup) of milk and squash mixture. Repeat layers two more times: noodles, mushrooms, squash, noodles, mushrooms, squash. Cover lasagna with aluminum foil and bake for 20 minutes. Remove foil and bake for another 10 minutes. Transfer to a wire rack to stand for 10 minutes before serving.

Serves 4–6

black bean & pumpkin stew

see variations page 223

Pumpkins aren't just for pies! Try this vegan dish once and you'll be hooked.

1 lb. pumpkin, peeled, seeds removed, and
   cubed
4 garlic cloves, minced
4 cups vegetable stock
1 tbsp. extra-virgin olive oil
2 cups finely chopped onion
2 cups seeded and chopped red bell pepper

2 tsp. dried basil
1 cup corn kernels, fresh or frozen
26 oz. black beans (2 cans), with liquid
1 tbsp. fresh lime juice
salt and freshly ground black pepper to taste
2 tbsp. finely chopped Italian parsley, to garnish

In a large saucepan over medium-high heat, cover pumpkin cubes and garlic with vegetable stock. Bring to a boil, reduce heat, cover, and simmer for 15–20 minutes, until pumpkin is tender. Using an immersion blender or food processor, purée pumpkin mixture. Set aside.

In a separate large saucepan, heat olive oil over medium-low heat. Add onions and peppers and sauté for 15 minutes, until they begin to caramelize. Add basil to the saucepan and stir. Transfer puréed pumpkin mixture to the saucepan and stir to combine. Stir in corn and black beans with liquid. Continue cooking over medium-low heat, stirring frequently, until heated through. Stir in lime juice and season to taste. Serve in bowls and garnish with parsley.

Serves 4

three-pepper casserole

see variations page 224

If you count the ground chili and the paprika, this is really a five-pepper casserole.

2 tbsp. unsalted butter
2 tbsp. extra-virgin olive oil
2 cups thinly sliced onions
2 garlic cloves, minced
1 tsp. salt
1 tsp. ground coriander
1 tsp. ground cumin
1/2 tsp. mustard powder
1/4 tsp. crushed red pepper flakes

2 green bell peppers, seeded and thinly sliced
2 yellow bell peppers, seeded and thinly sliced
2 red bell peppers, seeded and thinly sliced
2 tbsp. all-purpose flour
1 cup grated reduced-fat cheddar cheese
4 eggs
1 1/2 cups plain yogurt
pinch of Spanish paprika

Preheat oven to 375°F. In a large, heavy-based frying pan, heat butter and olive oil. Add onions and garlic, then stir in salt, coriander, cumin, mustard powder, and pepper flakes. Sauté for 5 minutes, until onions are translucent. Add sliced bell peppers and sauté for another 10 minutes, until peppers are tender. Add flour and stir until completely incorporated. Lightly butter a large casserole. Spread half the pepper mixture over the bottom of the dish. Sprinkle with half the grated cheese. Top with the remaining peppers, then with the remaining cheese.

In a medium bowl, whisk eggs and yogurt together. Pour egg mixture over casserole and sprinkle with paprika. Cover casserole with lid or aluminum foil, and bake for 40 minutes. Remove cover and cook for another 15 minutes, until casserole is bubbly and brown on top.

Serves 6

lentil & root vegetable casserole

see variations page 225

This hearty low-fat casserole is ready to serve in under an hour.

3 tbsp. extra-virgin olive oil
1/2 lb. rutabaga, peeled and diced
1/2 lb. parsnips, peeled and diced
1/2 lb. carrots, peeled and diced
2 celery stalks, chopped
2 cups finely chopped onions
3/4 cup dried brown or orange lentils

2 garlic cloves, minced
1 (14-oz.) can whole tomatoes with liquid
2 1/2 cups vegetable stock
salt and freshly ground black pepper to taste
2 tsp. fresh lemon juice
2 tbsp. finely chopped Italian parsley, to garnish

In a large, heavy-based saucepan or Dutch oven, heat oil over medium heat. Add rutabaga, parsnips, carrots, celery, and onions. Cook for 5 minutes, stirring occasionally. Add lentils and garlic and cook for another 5 minutes, stirring often. Add tomatoes, stock, and salt and pepper. Bring to a boil, reduce heat, cover, and simmer for 30–45 minutes, until lentils are soft. Stir in lemon juice. Serve in bowls and garnish with parsley.

Serves 4

yam, squash & pear casserole

see variations page 226

You won't miss the extra calories (or the marshmallows) in this lighter version of a Thanksgiving favorite. You could cook it in individual portion-sized dishes, if you prefer.

2 lb. yams, peeled and cubed
1 1/2 lb. butternut squash, peeled, seeds
    removed, and cubed
1 lb. pears, peeled, seeds removed, and cubed
2 tbsp. apple juice
1 banana, mashed
1/3 cup evaporated skim milk

1 tsp. ground cinnamon
1/2 tsp. ground nutmeg
1/4 tsp. ground cardamom
2 eggs
3/4 cups oats
1/4 cup brown sugar

In a large Dutch oven, cover yams and squash with water. Bring to boil, reduce heat, and simmer for 20 minutes, until soft. Drain and set aside. In a medium frying pan over medium-high heat, sauté pears in apple juice for 5–6 minutes, until tender. Transfer yams, squash, and pears to a food processor or large mixing bowl. Add banana, evaporated skim milk, cinnamon, nutmeg, cardamom, and eggs. Pulse or mash until smooth.

Preheat oven to 350°F. Lightly grease a large casserole (9x13x2-inch) with light cooking spray. Transfer yam mixture to casserole, smoothing top with spatula. Combine oats and sugar in a mixing bowl and sprinkle over yam mixture. Bake for 30 minutes, until heated through and topping is golden brown.

Serves 12

cauliflower & red pepper casserole

see variations page 227

Cauliflower and peppers complement each other beautifully in this gorgeous offering.
Cook and serve in individual portion-sized dishes as shown here, if you prefer.

low-fat cooking spray
1 large head of cauliflower, cut into florets
1 large red bell pepper, seeded and sliced
1 1/2 cups skim milk
3 tbsp. all-purpose flour
zest of 1 lemon
1 1/4 tsp. dried basil

1/2 tsp. salt
1/2 tsp. freshly ground black pepper
4 oz. light cream cheese, cubed
1 tbsp. non-hydrogenated margarine, melted
1 cup fresh whole wheat breadcrumbs
1/4 cup freshly grated Parmesan

Preheat oven to 375°F. Lightly coat a large casserole (9x13-inch) with low-fat cooking spray;
set aside. In a large pot of boiling water, cook cauliflower for 3 minutes, until crisp-tender.
Drain and place in prepared casserole. Sprinkle red bell pepper over cauliflower.

In a medium saucepan over medium heat, whisk milk, flour, lemon zest, 1 teaspoon basil,
salt, and black pepper. Bring mixture to a boil and cook until thickened, about 5 minutes.
Add cream cheese and whisk until completely incorporated. Pour sauce over cauliflower
and peppers.

In a small bowl, combine melted margarine, breadcrumbs, Parmesan, and remaining
1/4 tablespoon basil. Sprinkle over the casserole. Bake for 20 minutes, until bubbly and
golden. Transfer to wire rack to stand for 5 minutes before serving.

Serves 6–8

lemon chicken with kasha

see variations page 228

A lovely alternative to chicken and rice.

2 tsp. canola oil
6 skinless, boneless chicken breasts
salt and freshly ground black pepper to taste
1 1/2 cups finely chopped onions
2 garlic cloves, minced
1 1/2 cups kasha

1/2 tsp. ground cumin
1/2 tsp. ground coriander
1/2 tsp. ground cardamom
juice and zest from 1 lemon
3 cups fat-free low-sodium chicken broth

Preheat oven to 350°F. In a large, heavy-based frying pan, heat oil over medium heat. Add chicken and brown on both sides. Season with salt and pepper and transfer to a large (9x13-inch) casserole. Add onions to frying pan and sauté until soft and translucent, about 5 minutes. Add garlic and continue sautéing for 1 minute. Add kasha to frying pan, stirring to coat with the oil. Cook for 1 minute, stirring well. Add cumin, coriander, cardamom, and lemon juice and zest. Stir well, then spoon kasha mixture over chicken.

In a medium saucepan, bring chicken broth to a boil. Pour broth over kasha and chicken. Cover the casserole tightly with aluminum foil and bake for 45 minutes, until chicken is cooked through and kasha has absorbed almost all the chicken broth.

Serves 6

dijon turkey stew

see variations page 229

Dijon mustard and white wine make this turkey casserole worthy of company.

1 tbsp. extra-virgin olive oil, plus 1 tsp.
2 large leeks, julienned
3 garlic cloves, minced
1/3 cup all-purpose flour, plus 1 tbsp.
1 1/2 lb. skinless, boneless turkey breasts, cut
   into bite-sized pieces
1/2 tsp. salt
1/2 tsp. freshly ground black pepper

1 cup dry white wine
3 cups low-sodium turkey or chicken broth
1 1/2 cups water
2 tbsp. Dijon mustard
1 lb. russet potatoes, peeled and cut into
   1/2-inch pieces
3 carrots, roughly chopped
pinch of crushed red pepper flakes

Heat 1 teaspoon oil in Dutch oven over medium-high heat. Add leeks and sauté until golden brown and tender, about 6 minutes. Add garlic and continue cooking for 1 minute. Transfer leeks and garlic to a bowl and set aside.

Place 1/3 cup flour in shallow dish and dredge turkey pieces, shaking off excess. Heat remaining oil in Dutch oven and brown turkey on all sides, seasoning with a pinch of salt and pepper. Transfer browned turkey to the bowl with leek mixture. Pour wine into Dutch oven and deglaze. In a measuring cup, whisk 1 tablespoon flour into 1 cup turkey or chicken broth. When mixture is smooth, add to Dutch oven. Stir, then add remaining 2 cups broth, water, and mustard. Bring to a boil and return turkey and leek mixture to the pot. Stir in remaining salt and pepper, reduce heat, cover, and simmer for 30 minutes. Add potatoes and carrots, cover, and simmer for 30 more minutes. Serve with a pinch of crushed red pepper.

Serves 6

variations

zucchini & polenta bake

see base recipe page 205

zucchini, eggplant & polenta bake
Prepare the basic recipe, replacing 1 zucchini with 1 unpeeled medium eggplant, ends trimmed and diced.

zucchini & polenta bake with olives
Prepare the basic recipe, adding 1 cup pitted and chopped black olives to the tomato sauce before adding the basil.

zucchini, summer squash & polenta bake
Prepare the basic recipe, replacing 1 zucchini with 1 small summer squash.

zucchini, pepper & polenta bake
Prepare the basic recipe, adding 1 cup seeded and diced red bell pepper when sautéing the zucchini.

zucchini & polenta bake with taleggio
Prepare the basic recipe, replacing the part-skim mozzarella with an equal quantity of taleggio.

variations

butternut squash lasagna

see base recipe page 206

butternut squash lasagna with shiitake mushrooms
Prepare the basic recipe, replacing 1/2 cup of the cremini mushrooms with 1/2 cup shiitake mushrooms.

acorn squash lasagna
Prepare the basic recipe, replacing the butternut squash with an equal quantity of acorn squash.

butternut squash lasagna with oregano
Prepare the basic recipe, replacing the sage with 1/2 teaspoon dried oregano.

butternut squash lasagna with hazelnuts
Prepare the basic recipe, adding 1 cup toasted and finely chopped hazelnuts, with skins removed, to the squash and mushroom mixture.

butternut squash lasagna with spinach
Prepare the basic recipe, adding 2 cups roughly chopped fresh spinach leaves to the squash and mushroom mixture.

black bean & pumpkin stew

see base recipe page 209

black bean & butternut squash stew
Prepare the basic recipe, replacing the pumpkin with an equal quantity
of butternut squash.

pinto bean & pumpkin stew
Prepare the basic recipe, replacing the black beans with an equal quantity
of pinto beans.

kidney bean & pumpkin stew
Prepare the basic recipe, replacing the black beans with an equal quantity
of kidney beans.

black bean, pumpkin & chipotle stew
Prepare the basic recipe, adding 1/4 teaspoon chipotle chili powder with
the basil.

black bean, pumpkin & tomato stew
Prepare the basic recipe, adding 1 1/2 cups canned whole tomatoes, with
their liquid, to the onion mixture before adding the pumpkin and the corn.

variations

three-pepper casserole

see base recipe page 210

three-pepper casserole with jalapeño havarti
Prepare the basic recipe, replacing the reduced-fat cheddar with an equal amount of jalapeño Havarti.

three-pepper casserole with monterey jack
Prepare the basic recipe, replacing the reduced-fat cheddar with an equal amount of Monterey Jack.

three-pepper casserole with fresh cilantro
Prepare the basic recipe, garnishing each portion with 2 teaspoons chopped fresh cilantro.

three-pepper casserole with corn
Prepare the basic recipe, sprinkling 1/2 cup fresh or frozen corn kernels over each layer of pepper mixture (1 cup corn total).

three-pepper casserole with green beans
Prepare the basic recipe, adding 1 cup fresh green beans, in 1-inch pieces, with the peppers.

variations

lentil & root vegetable casserole

see base recipe page 213

barley & root vegetable casserole
Prepare the basic recipe, replacing the lentils with an equal quantity of barley.

quinoa & root vegetable casserole
Prepare the basic recipe, replacing the lentils with an equal quantity of quinoa.

lentil & root vegetable casserole with thyme
Prepare the basic recipe, adding 1/2 teaspoon dried thyme with the tomatoes.

lentil & root vegetable casserole with sweet potatoes
Prepare the basic recipe, adding 1 pound sweet potatoes, peeled and chopped, with the other root vegetables.

lentil & root vegetable casserole with fennel
Prepare the basic recipe, adding 1 fennel bulb, ends trimmed and roughly chopped, with the root vegetables.

variations

yam, squash & pear casserole

see base recipe page 214

lighter yam, squash & pear casserole
Prepare the basic recipe, omitting topping.

yam, squash & apple casserole
Prepare the basic recipe, replacing the pear with an equal quantity
of peeled and cubed apple.

granola-topped yam, squash & pear casserole
Prepare the basic recipe, replacing the oats with an equal quantity
of prepared granola.

yam, squash & pear casserole with raisins
Prepare the basic recipe, adding 1/2 cup raisins to the yam mixture after
it has been mashed.

variations

cauliflower & red pepper casserole

see base recipe page 217

broccoli & red pepper casserole
Prepare the basic recipe, replacing the cauliflower with an equal quantity
of broccoli florets.

cauliflower & red pepper casserole with feta
Prepare the basic recipe, replacing the cream cheese with an equal quantity
of crumbled feta.

cauliflower & red pepper casserole with sun-dried tomatoes
Prepare the basic recipe, adding 1/3 cup chopped sun-dried tomatoes with
the red pepper.

cauliflower & red pepper casserole with artichoke hearts
Prepare the basic recipe, adding 1/2 cup drained and chopped artichoke
hearts with the red pepper.

lemon chicken with kasha

see base recipe page 218

lemon chicken with barley
Prepare the basic recipe, replacing the kasha with an equal quantity
of barley.

lemon chicken with kasha & peas
Prepare the basic recipe, adding 1 cup fresh or frozen peas in the last
5 minutes of cooking.

lemon chicken with kasha & olives
Prepare the basic recipe, adding 1/2 cup pitted and halved kalamata olives
with the broth.

lemon turkey with kasha
Prepare the basic recipe, replacing the chicken breasts with an equal amount
of skinless, boneless turkey breast.

variations

dijon turkey stew

see base recipe page 220

dijon chicken stew
Prepare the basic recipe, replacing the turkey with an equal amount of skinless, boneless chicken breast.

grainy mustard turkey stew
Prepare the basic recipe, replacing the Dijon mustard with an equal quantity of grainy mustard.

tarragon mustard turkey stew
Prepare the basic recipe, replacing the Dijon mustard with an equal quantity of tarragon mustard.

dijon turkey stew with mango chutney
Prepare the basic recipe, adding 1/3 cup prepared mango chutney to the Dijon mustard before adding it to the stew.

quick & easy casseroles

When you need something filling fast, look to this chapter, with its recipes that can be on the table in 45 minutes or less, allowing you to have a healthy and delicious home-cooked meal, without a lot of effort and clean-up.

quick fish curry

see variations page 247

Simple and satisfying, this curry uses only one frying pan and is ready in a matter of minutes.

1 tbsp. canola oil
1 cup finely chopped onion
1 garlic clove, minced
1–2 tbsp. Madras curry paste

1 (14-oz.) can whole tomatoes, with liquid
3/4 cup vegetable broth
1 1/2 lb. cod fillet, skinned and cut into bite-sized pieces

In a large, heavy-based frying pan, heat oil over medium heat. Add onion and garlic and sauté until soft and translucent, about 5 minutes. Add curry paste and cook for another 2 minutes, stirring frequently. Stir in tomatoes and broth. Bring to a boil, then reduce heat to simmer. Add cod pieces and cook for 4–5 minutes, until fish is opaque and flakes easily.

Serves 4

hamburger stroganoff

see variations page 248

A speedy alternative to the classic stroganoff.

1 lb. lean ground beef
1 onion, finely chopped
1 garlic clove, minced
1 tbsp. Worcestershire sauce
1/2 tsp. salt
1/4 tsp. freshly ground black pepper

2 cans condensed cream of mushroom soup
1 1/2 cups milk
1 (8-oz.) can sliced mushrooms, drained
2 tsp. dry sherry
1 cup sour cream
2 tbsp. finely chopped Italian parsley, to garnish

In a large, heavy-based frying pan over medium-high heat, brown beef and onion, about 5–6 minutes. Add garlic and cook for 1 minute. Drain and stir in Worcestershire sauce, salt, and pepper. Add cream of mushroom soup and milk. Stir until well incorporated. Add mushrooms and cook until heated through, about 4–5 minutes. Stir in sherry and sour cream and cook for 2 minutes longer. Remove from heat and serve, garnished with parsley.

Serves 6

shortcut lasagna

see variations page 249

When you're craving lasagna but don't have time to make one, this is an excellent stand-in.

1 tbsp. olive oil
1 medium onion, sliced
2 cloves garlic, minced
1 medium red bell pepper, chopped
4 cups crushed canned tomatoes with liquid
2 tbsp. finely chopped fresh basil

1/2 tsp. dried oregano
salt and freshly ground black pepper to taste
1 1/2 lb. thin ripple-edged pasta such as
    reginette or mafaldine
2/3 cup grated mozzarella

Fill large saucepan with water and bring to boil. Heat olive oil in 10-inch nonstick frying pan. When oil is hot, add onion, garlic, and red bell pepper. Sauté for 10 minutes, until onion is soft and brown. Add tomatoes, basil, and oregano, and simmer for 5 minutes. Add salt and pepper to taste.

Place pasta in salted boiling water and cook for 9 minutes. Drain and add to frying pan. Taking care to blend pasta and sauce thoroughly, cook for 10 minutes, until tomato sauce thickens and coats pasta evenly. Remove from heat and arrange grated mozzarella over pasta. Cover frying pan for several minutes to allow cheese to melt.

Serves 4

spinach & cremini mushroom casserole

see variations page 250

The combination of spinach and mushrooms always pleases.

2 tbsp. unsalted butter
1 cup sliced cremini mushrooms
1 garlic clove, minced
1 tbsp. fresh lemon juice
18 oz. fresh spinach
1 cup ricotta cheese
1/4 tsp. dried oregano

1/2 tsp. salt
1/4 tsp. freshly ground black pepper
pinch of ground nutmeg
6–8 fresh tomato slices
1 cup grated mozzarella
1/4 cup grated Parmesan

Preheat oven to 350°F. Melt butter in a medium frying pan over medium heat. Add mushrooms and garlic and sauté for 5 minutes, until soft. Remove from heat, add lemon juice, stir, and set aside.

Rinse spinach and drain. Place spinach in a large saucepan and allow to steam for a few minutes in the moisture remaining on the leaves, just until all the spinach has wilted. Drain again and chop. Place spinach in a large bowl. Add ricotta, oregano, salt, and pepper, and the mushroom mixture. Mix well. Transfer spinach mixture to a lightly buttered casserole. Arrange tomato slices over spinach mixture, sprinkle with mozzarella, then with Parmesan, and bake for 30 minutes, until heated through and golden brown on top.

Serves 4

potato & tomato frittata

see variations page 251

This quick egg and potato dish can be served at any time of day.

1 lb. new potatoes, quartered
1 tbsp. extra-virgin olive oil
1 garlic clove, minced

3/4 cup halved cherry tomatoes
8 eggs, beaten
salt and freshly ground black pepper to taste

Place potatoes in a large pot of lightly salted water, bring to a boil, and cook for 8–10 minutes, until tender. Drain. Heat oil in a large ovenproof frying pan over medium-low heat. Add garlic and cook for 1 minute.

Preheat broiler. Transfer potatoes to frying pan, add tomatoes, and pour eggs over everything. Sprinkle with salt and pepper. Cook until bottom is set (you can lift the bottom easily with a spatula), about 5 minutes, then transfer pan to broiler and cook for another 3 minutes, until top is set and beginning to brown. Serve in wedges.

Serves 4

leftover turkey casserole

see variations page 252

Don't let your Thanksgiving or Christmas leftovers sit forgotten in the fridge. Assemble this casserole in minutes and enjoy an easy feast.

2 cups chopped cooked turkey
2 cups leftover steamed or roasted vegetables
1 cup leftover or canned turkey gravy

2 cups leftover stuffing or mashed potatoes
freshly ground black pepper to taste

Preheat oven to 350°F. In a large mixing bowl, combine leftover turkey and vegetables. Toss with leftover gravy. Pour turkey mixture into an 8x8-inch casserole. Spread leftover stuffing or mashed potatoes or a combination of both over the turkey mixture. Sprinkle with black pepper and bake for 20–25 minutes, until heated through.

Serves 4

quinoa casserole

see variations page 253

Quinoa is a gluten-free grain, making this quick dish a perfect choice to serve guests with celiac disease.

12 oz. quinoa
3 cups water
3 tbsp. extra-virgin olive oil
1 cup finely chopped onion
1 yellow bell pepper, seeded and chopped

1 bunch rapini, chopped
3 garlic cloves, minced
1 cup sliced mushrooms
1/4 cup finely chopped Italian parsley, to
    garnish

Rinse quinoa well, then place in large saucepan with water. Stir, cover, and cook over medium-low heat for 15 minutes, until soft and liquid is absorbed.

While quinoa is cooking, heat 2 tablespoons oil in a large frying pan over medium heat. Add onion and bell pepper and sauté for 5 minutes, until onion is soft and translucent. Add rapini and garlic and sauté for 2 minutes longer. In a separate small frying pan, heat remaining oil over medium heat. Add mushrooms and sauté for 5 minutes, until tender. Once quinoa is cooked (all the liquid should be absorbed), combine it with the rapini mixture and the mushrooms. Stir to combine and serve, garnished with parsley.

Serves 8

broccoli–artichoke bake

see variations page 254

This is a lovely way to dress up broccoli.

3 cups broccoli florets
14 oz. artichoke hearts, drained and halved
3 tbsp. unsalted butter
1/4 cup finely chopped onion
3 tbsp. all-purpose flour

salt and freshly ground black pepper to taste
2 1/2 cups whole milk
1 cup soft breadcrumbs
2 tbsp. unsalted butter, melted
1/4 cup grated Parmesan

Preheat oven to 350°F. Steam broccoli florets for 6 minutes, until tender-crisp. Drain and place in a lightly buttered medium casserole. Add halved artichoke hearts and gently toss.

To prepare the sauce, melt butter in large saucepan over low heat. Add chopped onion and sauté until translucent, about 5 minutes. Add flour, salt, and pepper. Stir constantly, until mixture is smooth and bubbling. Continue stirring for 1 minute, then remove from heat. Whisk in milk and return to stove. Bring mixture to boil, whisking continuously. Remove from heat once mixture has thickened, about 1–2 minutes after it comes to a boil. Pour sauce over broccoli and artichoke mixture.

In a medium bowl, combine breadcrumbs, melted butter, and Parmesan. Spread over casserole. Bake for 30–40 minutes, until heated through and bubbly.

Serves 4–6

cottage pie

see variations page 255

Cottage pie is the name given to a shepherd's pie made with ground beef instead of lamb. It is a traditional British dish.

2 lb. lean ground beef, browned and drained
1 tbsp. steak spice
freshly ground black pepper to taste
1 cup canned or frozen corn kernels
4–5 large russet potatoes

6 tbsp. butter
1/2 cup whole milk
1/4 tsp. salt
1 tbsp. chopped fresh Italian parsley, to garnish

Preheat oven to 375°F. Spread cooked beef over bottom of buttered large (13x9x2-inch) baking dish. Sprinkle steak spice and black pepper over beef. Spread corn on top.

To make mashed potatoes, peel and halve russet potatoes. Place in large saucepan and cover with water. Bring to boil and cook for 20 minutes, or until potatoes begin to fall apart when pricked with fork. Drain potatoes and beat for a few seconds on low, using electric beater or standing mixer. Add butter, milk, salt, and pepper and beat on medium-high until potatoes are light and creamy.

Spread mashed potatoes over filling. Bake pie for 20 minutes, or until filling is hot and potatoes are lightly browned. Garnish with chopped parsley before serving.

Serves 6–8

variations

quick fish curry

see base recipe page 231

quick fish curry with peas
Prepare the basic recipe, adding 1 cup fresh or frozen peas with the cod.

quick sole curry
Prepare the basic recipe, replacing the cod with an equal quantity of sole.

quick fish korma
Prepare the basic recipe, replacing the Madras curry paste with an equal
quantity of a milder, korma paste.

quick fish curry with pepper
Prepare the basic recipe, adding 1 cup seeded and chopped red bell pepper
with the tomatoes.

quick fish curry with fresh cilantro
Prepare the basic recipe, adding 1/4 cup finely chopped fresh cilantro with
the tomatoes.

variations

hamburger stroganoff

see base recipe page 232

lighter hamburger stroganoff
Prepare the basic recipe, replacing the lean ground beef with extra-lean ground beef, the cream of mushroom soup with reduced-fat condensed mushroom soup, and the sour cream with fat-free plain yogurt.

hamburger stroganoff with green pepper
Prepare the basic recipe, adding 1 cup seeded and chopped green bell pepper with the onions.

turkey stroganoff
Prepare the basic recipe, replacing the lean ground beef with an equal quantity of lean ground turkey.

hamburger stroganoff with portobello mushrooms
Prepare the basic recipe, adding 6 ounces fresh portobello mushrooms, cleaned and sliced into thin strips, with the onions.

hamburger stroganoff with broad egg noodles
Prepare the basic recipe. As the meat and onions are sautéing, bring a pot of water to a boil. Cook 2 cups broad egg noodles according to package instructions. Drain and stir into stroganoff when it has been removed from the burner.

variations

shortcut lasagna

see base recipe page 235

shortcut lasagna with ricotta
Prepare the basic recipe, folding 1 cup ricotta into the sauce when adding the pasta noodles.

shortcut lasagna with corn & cumin
Prepare the basic recipe, omitting basil and oregano. Add 1 teaspoon ground cumin, 1/2 teaspoon ground coriander, and 1 cup fresh or frozen corn kernels with the tomatoes.

shortcut linguine
Prepare the basic recipe, replacing the rippled-edged noodles with an equal quantity of linguine. Reduce cooking time for noodles to 5 minutes.

shortcut lasagna with sautéed mushrooms
Prepare the basic recipe, adding 1 cup sliced cremini mushrooms with the onion.

shortcut lasagna with zucchini
Prepare the basic recipe, adding 1 small zucchini, diced, with the onion.

spinach & cremini mushroom casserole

see base recipe page 236

spinach, mushroom & bacon casserole
Prepare the basic recipe, adding 4–5 bacon slices (which have been fried until crispy, drained, and crumbled) to the spinach mixture before transferring to casserole dish.

spinach, mushroom & artichoke casserole
Prepare the basic recipe, adding 1 cup drained and roughly chopped artichoke hearts to the spinach mixture before transferring to casserole dish.

spinach, mushroom & lentil casserole
Prepare the basic recipe, adding 1 cup drained cooked or canned lentils to the spinach mixture before transferring to casserole dish.

spicy spinach & mushroom casserole
Prepare the basic recipe, adding 1/4 or 1/2 teaspoon hot pepper sauce to the spinach mixture before transferring to casserole dish.

spinach, mushroom & roasted red pepper casserole
Prepare the basic recipe, adding 1 cup prepared roasted red bell peppers, which have been drained and roughly chopped, to the spinach mixture before transferring to casserole dish.

variations

potato & tomato frittata

see base recipe page 239

potato, tomato & arugula frittata
Prepare the basic recipe, adding 1 ounce arugula, roughly chopped, to the frying pan with the tomatoes, and garnishing with 1 more ounce just before serving.

potato, tomato & olive frittata
Prepare the basic recipe, adding 3 ounces pitted and chopped black olives to the frying pan with the tomatoes.

potato, tomato & ham frittata
Prepare the basic recipe, adding 1/2 cup cubed smoked ham to the frying pan with the tomatoes.

lighter potato & tomato frittata
Prepare the basic recipe, replacing the 8 eggs with 10 egg whites.

variations

leftover turkey casserole

see base recipe page 240

leftover roast chicken casserole

Prepare the basic recipe, replacing the leftover turkey with an equal quantity of leftover roast chicken.

leftover turkey casserole with caramelized onions

Prepare the basic recipe, adding 1 cup sliced onions that have been sautéed in 2 tablespoons unsalted butter until caramelized, 12–15 minutes. Toss caramelized onions with turkey before proceeding with recipe.

leftover turkey casserole with lentils

Prepare the basic recipe, adding 1 cup drained cooked or canned lentils. Toss lentils with the turkey before proceeding with recipe.

leftover turkey with biscuits

Prepare the basic recipe, omitting stuffing and mashed potatoes. Preheat oven to 400°F. Prepare biscuits following package directions. Arrange biscuits over turkey mixture and cook for 18–20 minutes, until biscuits are cooked and turkey mixture is heated through.

variations

quinoa casserole

see base recipe page 243

quinoa casserole with sunflower seeds
Prepare the basic recipe, garnishing each serving with 2 tablespoons toasted sunflower seeds.

mixed quinoa casserole
Prepare the basic recipe, replacing half the white quinoa with red quinoa.

bulgur casserole
Prepare the basic recipe, replacing the quinoa with an equal quantity of bulgur. Prepare bulgur according to package instructions before proceeding with recipe.

quinoa casserole with raisins
Prepare the basic recipe, adding 1/4 cup raisins to the quinoa mixture when combining with rapini and mushrooms.

broccoli–artichoke bake

see base recipe page 244

cauliflower–artichoke bake
Prepare the basic recipe, replacing the broccoli with an equal quantity of cauliflower florets.

broccoli, artichoke & hearts of palm bake
Prepare the basic recipe, adding 1/2 cup hearts of palm to the mixture with the artichoke hearts.

broccoli–artichoke bake with chèvre
Prepare the basic recipe, adding 5 ounces crumbled chèvre to the sauce before pouring over the vegetable mixture.

broccoli, artichoke & sun-dried tomato bake
Prepare the basic recipe, adding 1/2 cup roughly chopped sun-dried tomatoes to the mixture with the artichoke hearts.

cottage pie

see base recipe page 246

shepherd's pie
Prepare the basic recipe, replacing ground beef with an equal quantity of ground lamb, browned and drained.

cottage pie with green peas
Prepare the basic recipe, replacing the corn with 1 cup fresh or frozen peas.

vegetarian cottage pie
Prepare the basic recipe, replacing the ground beef with 4 cups prepared textured vegetable protein (TVP).

cottage pie with ricotta topping
Prepare the basic recipe, omitting the mashed potato topping. In large bowl, combine 2 cups ricotta cheese, 2 eggs, 1/2 teaspoon dried oregano, and 1/3 cup grated mozzarella cheese. Spread cheese topping over filling and bake for 20 minutes or until filling is hot and cheese is golden brown.

cottage pie with parsnips
Prepare the basic recipe, using only 2 large russet potatoes and adding 4 large parsnips. Peel, quarter, remove tough center, and chop parsnips. Boil potatoes and parsnips for 20 minutes and proceed with recipe.

international favorites

In this chapter you can experiment with the flavors

of faraway cuisines and be sure that your culinary

explorations will be met with enthusiasm each time.

moroccan tagine

see variations page 273

An aromatic and succulent way to prepare chicken. If you don't have a tagine (an earthenware dish from North Africa), you can prepare this dish on top of the stove.

2 tbsp. extra-virgin olive oil
2 lb. boneless, skinless chicken breasts, cut into
    bite-sized pieces
1/2 onion, finely chopped
3 cloves garlic, minced
2 carrots, chopped
1 (14-oz.) can whole tomatoes with liquid

1 (15-oz.) can chickpeas, drained and rinsed
1 1/2 cups vegetable broth
1 tbsp. lemon juice
1 tbsp. sugar
1 tsp. salt
1 tsp. ground coriander
pinch of cayenne pepper

Heat oil in a large frying pan over medium heat. Add chicken and onion. Brown all over for 12 minutes, stirring occasionally, . Add garlic and continue cooking for 2 minutes. Stir in carrots, tomatoes with liquid, chickpeas, and broth. Add lemon juice, sugar, salt, coriander, and cayenne. Bring to a boil, reduce heat, cover, and simmer for 30 minutes, until chicken is cooked through and vegetables are tender.

(If using an authentic tagine, transfer mixture to the tagine after it comes to a boil. Bake in a preheated 375°F oven for 30–40 minutes.)

Serves 4–6

pot-au-feu

see variations page 274

This casserole is worth the added effort. It will give you two courses for your meal — an appetizer of marrow to spread on toasted baguette, and a stew of tender meat and vegetables. This recipe requires kitchen twine and cheesecloth.

2 lb. beef shank, with bone
2 lb. stewing beef, in one piece
2 lb. beef ribs
2 lb. large marrowbones
1 large onion, peeled
4 cloves
2 sprigs fresh thyme
2 bay leaves
2 celery stalks with leaves
6 sprigs fresh Italian parsley

1 tbsp. coarse sea salt
1 tsp. freshly ground black pepper
10 carrots, peeled and roughly chopped
8 leeks, cleaned, tough ends removed, cut in
    half lengthwise, and then in 1-inch pieces
1 1/2 lb. turnips, peeled and roughly chopped
1 1/2 lb. new potatoes
1 baguette, sliced thinly and toasted,
    for serving

Using kitchen twine, tie beef shank, stewing beef, and ribs together. Place in large Dutch oven. Wrap marrowbones in cheesecloth, tie with kitchen twine, and add to Dutch oven. Cover ingredients with water and place over medium-high heat. Bring water to a boil, then reduce heat to low, and let simmer. Stud onion with cloves and add to Dutch oven. Wrap thyme, bay leaves, celery stalks, and parsley in cheesecloth to make a bouquet garni. Add to Dutch oven with salt, pepper, carrots, leeks, and turnips. Simmer for 40 minutes. Add potatoes and simmer for another 20 minutes, until they are tender.

Untie and unwrap meats and place on a large platter. Place marrow bones on a separate plate and set aside. Arrange cooked vegetables around meats. Cover with aluminum foil and keep warm. Spoon marrow out of bones and spread on toasted baguette slices. Serve as an appetizer while you prepare the broth reduction, or save to serve alongside meats and vegetables. Discard onion and strain cooking liquid through cheesecloth into a medium saucepan. Place saucepan over medium-high heat and bring to a boil. Simmer for 15 minutes, until broth is slightly reduced. Place in serving dish and serve with meats and vegetables.

Serves 6–8

jambalaya

see variations page 275

A classic of Louisiana Creole cuisine, jambalaya can even be made with alligator meat!

2 tbsp. canola oil
1 lb. boneless chicken, cubed
salt and freshly ground black pepper to taste
1 lb. andouille sausage, sliced into bite-sized
    chunks
1 onion, finely chopped
1 red bell pepper, seeded and finely chopped
4 celery stalks, finely chopped
4 garlic cloves, minced
18 oz. tomato paste

1 (28-oz.) can whole tomatoes with liquid
8 cups low-sodium chicken broth
2 tsp. cayenne pepper
2 tsp. freshly ground black pepper
1 tsp. ground white pepper
1 tsp. dried oregano
1/2 tsp. dried thyme
2 bay leaves
4 cups uncooked long-grain rice
1 lb. cooked, peeled shrimp

In a large Dutch oven, heat 1 tablespoon oil over medium-high heat. When oil is shimmering, add chicken cubes, season with salt and pepper, and brown on all sides, about 4 minutes per side. Transfer to plate and set aside. Add sausage to Dutch oven and brown, about 3 minutes per side. Transfer to plate with chicken. Heat remaining 1 tablespoon oil and sauté onion, bell pepper, and celery for 5 minutes, until onion is soft and translucent. Add garlic and cook for 1 minute. Add tomato paste and stir until color deepens to a brownish-red. Add tomatoes and 2 cups broth and deglaze Dutch oven, scraping any sticky bits and stirring until smooth. Add cayenne, ground peppers, oregano, thyme, and bay leaves. Return chicken and sausage to pot and add remaining broth and rice. Stir, cover, and cook for 20–25 minutes, until rice is tender and has absorbed almost all the liquid. Reduce heat to medium-low, add shrimp, and cook for another 10 minutes, until shrimp is heated and sauce has thickened a bit more.

Serves 6–8

easy cassoulet

see variations page 276

Authentic cassoulet can be a daunting project, involving expensive ingredients and lengthy preparation. This easy version conveys all the flavors of the original dish without quite as much effort. Be sure to begin soaking your beans the night before you plan to make your cassoulet.

1 1/2 cups dried white beans (white haricot beans), soaked in water overnight
10 oz. pork belly, rind discarded, thinly sliced
5 oz. thick-sliced bacon, cut into 1/2-inch pieces
2 lb. boned lamb shoulder, cut into 1 1/2-inch chunks
1 large onion, finely chopped
1 leek, cleaned, white and pale green part julienned

2 cloves garlic, minced
1 (14-oz.) can whole tomatoes with liquid
3 sprigs fresh thyme
2 bay leaves
1 cup water
1 cup low-sodium chicken broth
2 cups dry breadcrumbs
1/3 cup finely chopped Italian parsley

Preheat oven to 375°F. Drain beans and rinse until water runs clear. Place in a medium saucepan, cover with water, bring to a boil, and cook for 15 minutes, until tender. Drain and set aside. In a large Dutch oven over medium heat, brown pork slices, about 3 minutes. Transfer to plate and set aside. Cook bacon in Dutch oven until crisp, about 7–8 minutes. Transfer to plate with browned pork. Brown lamb in batches in pork and bacon fat, about 4 minutes per side. Transfer to another plate and set aside.

Drain fat from Dutch oven, leaving only 2 tablespoons. Cook onion and leek over medium-low heat for 4 minutes, until soft and translucent. Add garlic and continue cooking for

1 minute. Add tomatoes with their liquid, breaking them up into smaller pieces with a wooden spoon. Add thyme, bay leaves, water, and broth. Return meats to Dutch oven, raise heat, and bring to a boil. Cover and transfer to preheated oven. Cook for 45 minutes.

In a medium mixing bowl, combine breadcrumbs with chopped parsley. Remove casserole from oven, discard thyme sprigs and bay leaves if desired, sprinkle with breadcrumb mixture, and return to oven, uncovered. Cook for an additional 45 minutes, or until liquid is almost completely absorbed.

Serves 4–6

hungarian goulash

see variations page 277

The secret to authentic Hungarian goulash is lots of Hungarian paprika. Start with 2 tablespoons and add more to taste.

2 lb. stewing beef, cut into 1-inch cubes
1 tsp. salt, plus a pinch
2 tbsp. canola oil or shortening
2 onions, chopped
2 tbsp. Hungarian paprika
2 bay leaves

4 cups water
4 white potatoes, peeled and diced
1/4 tsp. freshly ground black pepper
6 tbsp. all-purpose flour
1 egg
sour cream, to garnish

Sprinkle beef with 1/2 teaspoon salt. Set aside. Heat oil or shortening in large Dutch oven over medium heat. Add onions and sauté for 5 minutes, until soft and translucent. Add beef, paprika, and bay leaves and cook until beef is browned on all sides, about 8 minutes. Reduce heat and simmer for 1 hour. Add water, potatoes, pepper, and 1/2 teaspoon salt. Cover and cook for 20–30 minutes, until potatoes are cooked and meat is tender.

To prepare egg dumplings, whisk flour and pinch of salt into egg in a small mixing bowl. Set aside for 30 minutes. Drop teaspoons of the mixture onto the goulash. Once dumplings have risen to the surface, cover and simmer for 5 minutes. Serve in bowls and garnish with sour cream.

Serves 6

lamb moussaka

see variations page 278

Serve this flavorful Greek dish with hunks of crusty bread for soaking up the sauce.

1 1/2 lb. zucchini
3 tbsp. extra-virgin olive oil
1 large onion, finely chopped
1 lb. ground lamb
2 cloves garlic, minced
1 piece of cinnamon
1 1/2 tsp. dried oregano
1 (10-oz.) package frozen spinach, thawed and
   drained

10 oz. prepared tomato sauce
1 cube organic chicken bouillon
salt and freshly ground black pepper to taste
2 tbsp. unsalted butter
1/4 cup all-purpose flour
1 1/2 cups milk
pinch of freshly grated nutmeg
2 tsp. lemon zest
1/3 cup freshly grated Parmesan

Preheat oven to broil. Slice zucchini into 1/2-inch slices. Spread in one layer on large oiled baking sheet. Drizzle with 1 tablespoon olive oil. Broil under the broiler for 5 minutes. Turn zucchini slices over and broil for 5 more minutes. Transfer to paper towel–lined rack to drain. Reduce oven temperature to 350°F.

To prepare the meat sauce, heat remaining 2 tablespoons olive oil over medium-low heat in large frying pan. Add onion to frying pan. Once onion is translucent, add ground lamb and cook until browned. Add garlic, cinnamon, oregano, spinach, tomato sauce, and bouillon cube. Break up bouillon cube until dissolved. Simmer for 10 minutes, stirring occasionally. Remove from heat. Remove and discard piece of cinnamon. Season to taste.

To prepare the béchamel sauce, melt butter over low heat in small saucepan. Add the flour and stir until you have a paste that is turning a reddish-brown (roux). Add the milk and whisk continuously until sauce thickens, 5–10 minutes. Whisk in the nutmeg and lemon zest and set aside. To assemble casserole, spread meat sauce over the base of a large, rectangular (2-quart) casserole. Layer zucchini slices over the sauce. Cover with béchamel sauce and sprinkle with Parmesan. Bake for 20–25 minutes until golden.

Serves 4–6

irish stew

see variations page 279

This recipe for Irish stew uses lamb chops, because the bones enhance the flavor of the finished dish.

4 lamb chops, 1 inch thick, rack end preferred
4 carrots, peeled and chopped
3 onions, roughly chopped
salt and freshly ground black pepper to taste
1/2 tsp. dried thyme
1 tsp. Worcestershire sauce

1 1/2 cups lamb or beef broth
4 russet potatoes, peeled and cubed
1/4 cup unsalted butter
1/4 cup all-purpose flour
2 tbsp. finely chopped curly parsley, to garnish

Preheat oven to 350°F. Trim some fat off the lamb chops and place the fat in a large, heavy-based frying pan. Cook for 5–8 minutes over medium heat, then remove and discard any pieces. Place lamb chops in the rendered fat in the hot frying pan and lightly brown, about 2 minutes per side. Transfer chops to a large casserole dish. Place carrots and onions over the lamb. Season with salt, pepper, thyme, and Worcestershire sauce. Pour broth over lamb and vegetables. Place potato cubes on top and season with more salt and pepper. Cover casserole and bake for 1 3/4 hours.

A few minutes before taking the stew out of the oven, make a roux by melting the butter in a medium saucepan over medium heat. Whisk in flour and cook for 2 minutes, whisking constantly, until mixture turns a light brown. Remove casserole from oven and pour most of the liquid from the dish into the pot with the roux. Whisk over medium heat to make a smooth gravy. Pour the gravy into the casserole and garnish with parsley.

Serves 4

italian risotto with scallops

see variations page 280

This exquisite risotto uses a zucchini purée to add a delicate flavor that perfectly complements the scallops.

1 pint cherry tomatoes
4 tbsp. extra-virgin olive oil, plus 2 tsp.
salt and freshly ground black pepper to taste
3/4 cup diced onion
1 garlic clove, minced
2 cups diced zucchini

1/4 cup fresh lemon juice
1 lb. uncooked Arborio rice
2–3 cups low-sodium chicken broth
1/4 cup grated Parmesan
18 medium scallops
1/4 cup finely chopped parsley, to garnish

Preheat oven to 250°F. Toss cherry tomatoes in 2 teaspoons oil. Season with salt and pepper, transfer to a lightly greased baking sheet, and roast for 1 hour. Set aside. Heat 1 tablespoon oil in a frying pan over medium heat. Add onion and cook for 4 minutes, stirring frequently. Add garlic and cook for 1 minute. Add zucchini and cook for 5 minutes more. Add lemon juice and 1 tablespoon oil, and purée the mixture, using an immersion blender or food processor. Set aside. To prepare the risotto, heat 1 tablespoon oil in a medium pot over medium heat. Add rice and stir to coat. Stir in 1 cup of broth at a time, stirring almost constantly until all the liquid is absorbed and rice is tender. Add zucchini purée and Parmesan and stir until well incorporated. Keep warm. Heat remaining tablespoon of oil in large frying pan. Add scallops, season with salt and pepper, and add roasted tomatoes. Sauté for 5–6 minutes, until scallops are opaque and beginning to brown. Fold scallops and tomatoes into risotto. Garnish each serving with parsley.

Serves 4

flemish carbonnade

see variations page 281

This classic Belgian stew takes its name from the French term for meat cooked over hot coals.

1/4 cup shortening or bacon drippings
3 lb. stewing beef, cubed and excess fat
    removed
3 cups sliced onions
2 garlic cloves, minced
salt and freshly ground black pepper to taste
24 fl oz. Belgian beer

1 cup beef broth
2 tbsp. brown sugar
1 bay leaf
1/2 tsp. dried thyme
1 tbsp. finely chopped Italian parsley
2 tbsp. all-purpose flour
1/2 cup water

Preheat oven to 325°F. Melt shortening or bacon drippings in large heatproof casserole over medium-high heat. Brown meat on all sides, about 10 minutes. Transfer to bowl and set aside. Add onions to casserole and sauté until soft and golden brown, about 8 minutes. Add garlic and cook for 2 minutes more. Season with salt and pepper, then add beer and beef broth. Return meat to casserole. The liquid should cover meat completely; if not, add water. Stir in brown sugar, bay leaf, thyme, and parsley. Cover, transfer to oven, and bake for 1 1/2 hours.

In a small bowl, whisk flour into water. Add flour mixture to casserole, stirring to combine. Return to stovetop and cook over medium heat for 15 minutes, stirring occasionally. Remove bay leaf and serve.

Serves 6

moroccan tagine

see base recipe page 257

moroccan lamb tagine
Prepare the basic recipe, replacing the chicken with an equal quantity of cubed boneless lamb.

moroccan pork tagine
Prepare the basic recipe, replacing the chicken with an equal quantity of cubed pork tenderloin.

moroccan beef tagine
Prepare the basic recipe, replacing the chicken with an equal quantity of cubed stewing beef.

moroccan tagine with currant couscous
Prepare the basic recipe, serving it with currant couscous (page 192).

moroccan tagine with almonds
Prepare the basic recipe, garnishing each serving with 2 tablespoons almond slivers.

variations

pot-au-feu

see base recipe page 258

pot-au-feu with grainy mustard

Prepare the basic recipe, spreading each baguette toast with 1/4 teaspoon grainy mustard before adding the soft marrow.

pot-au-feu with horseradish

Prepare the basic recipe, spreading each baguette toast with 1/4 teaspoon horseradish.

pot-au-feu with cinnamon

Prepare the basic recipe, adding 1 cinnamon stick with the other herbs and spices.

pot-au-feu with pork ribs

Prepare the basic recipe, replacing the beef ribs with an equal quantity of pork ribs.

pot-au-feu with cornichons

Prepare the basic recipe, garnishing each baguette toast with a cornichon.

variations

jambalaya

see base recipe page 261

jambalaya with ham
Prepare the basic recipe, replacing the shrimp with an equal quantity of cubed smoked ham.

jambalaya with creole seasoning
Prepare the basic recipe, replacing the cayenne, black and white peppers, thyme, and oregano with 2 teaspoons prepared Creole seasoning.

jambalaya with pasta
Prepare the basic recipe, omitting rice. Use only 4 cups of broth and only 12 ounces tomato paste. Cook 1 pound rigatoni according to package directions. Toss pasta with jambalaya, transfer to a large casserole, and bake in a preheated 350°F oven for 10–15 minutes.

jambalaya with snapper
Prepare the basic recipe, replacing the chicken with an equal quantity of snapper fillets, skinned and cut into bite-sized pieces.

turkey jambalaya
Prepare the basic recipe, replacing the chicken with an equal quantity of skinless, boneless turkey breast, cut into bite-sized pieces.

variations

easy cassoulet

see base recipe page 262

cassoulet with duck confit
Prepare the basic recipe, adding duck confit. To prepare the duck, preheat oven to 400°F. Arrange 6 duck confit legs in a baking dish and roast for 15 minutes. Remove meat from bones in large pieces, then cut into strips. Discard bones. Reduce oven temperature to 375°F. Arrange duck pieces over cassoulet before adding the breadcrumbs and proceed with recipe.

cassoulet with chickpeas
Prepare the basic recipe, replacing the haricot beans with dried chickpeas.

cassoulet with pancetta
Prepare the basic recipe, replacing the bacon with cubed pancetta.

cassoulet with cloves
Prepare the basic recipe, adding another onion, quartered, and studding each quarter with a clove.

cassoulet with merquez sausage
Prepare the basic recipe, adding 1 pound Merquez sausage, cut into 1-inch chunks. Brown Merquez with the other meats, about 3 minutes per side. Set aside and return to Dutch oven with the other meats.

hungarian goulash

see base recipe page 265

hungarian goulash with carrots
Prepare the basic recipe, adding 3–4 peeled and roughly chopped carrots with the potatoes.

hungarian goulash with tomatoes
Prepare the basic recipe, reducing the amount of water to 3 cups. Add 1 (14-ounce) can whole tomatoes with liquid when adding water and potatoes.

hungarian goulash with peppers
Prepare the basic recipe, adding 1 seeded and cubed red bell pepper with the onion.

hungarian goulash with olives
Prepare the basic recipe, adding 5 ounces pimiento-stuffed olives before adding the dumplings.

smoky hungarian goulash
Prepare the basic recipe, replacing 1 tablespoon of the Hungarian paprika with smoked paprika.

variations

lamb moussaka

see base recipe page 266

beef moussaka
Prepare the basic recipe, replacing the ground lamb with an equal quantity of lean ground beef.

vegetarian moussaka
Prepare the basic recipe, replacing the ground lamb with an equal quantity of prepared textured vegetable protein (TVP).

lamb moussaka with breadcrumbs
Prepare the basic recipe, topping the casserole with 1/2 cup breadcrumbs tossed with 2 tablespoons melted unsalted butter and 1/4 cup grated Parmesan.

lamb moussaka with eggplant
Prepare the basic recipe, replacing 1/2 pound sliced zucchini with 1/2 pound unpeeled sliced eggplant.

variations

irish stew

see base recipe page 269

irish stew with rutabaga
Prepare the basic recipe, adding 1 small peeled and cubed rutabaga with the potato.

irish stew with peas
Prepare the basic recipe, adding 1 cup fresh or frozen peas with the carrots.

irish stew with celery
Prepare the basic recipe, adding 2 chopped celery stalks with the carrots.

irish beef stew
Prepare the basic recipe, replacing the lamb with 1 1/2 pounds cubed stewing beef.

variations

italian risotto with scallops

see base recipe page 270

italian risotto with prawns
Prepare the basic recipe, replacing the scallops with 1 1/2 pounds shelled
and deveined prawns. Sauté prawns until they are pink and opaque.

italian risotto with clams
Prepare the basic recipe, replacing the scallops with 2 cups cooked clams.
Omit the sautéing step.

italian risotto with scallops & cauliflower
Prepare the basic recipe, adding 1 head of cauliflower, cut into florets, to the
cherry tomatoes for roasting. Add 1 tablespoon oil for tossing the vegetables
before roasting.

italian risotto with scallops & st. agur
Prepare the basic recipe, replacing the grated Parmesan with 4 ounces
crumbled St. Agur cheese.

flemish carbonnade

see base recipe page 272

flemish carbonnade with parsnips
Prepare the basic recipe, adding 2 peeled and roughly chopped parsnips
when returning casserole to stovetop for last 15 minutes of cooking.

flemish carbonnade with bacon
Prepare the basic recipe, beginning by frying 4–5 slices of bacon in casserole.
When bacon is crisp, 6–8 minutes, transfer to a plate and set aside. Omit
shortening, and proceed to browning beef in bacon drippings. Add bacon,
broken up, when returning beef to the casserole.

flemish carbonnade with croutons
Prepare the basic recipe, garnishing each serving with 1/4 cup croutons.

flemish carbonnade with dijon mustard
Prepare the basic recipe, adding 1 teaspoon Dijon mustard to the casserole
before adding the flour and water mixture.

index